VOICES OF RESISTANCE

DIARIES OF GENOCIDE

BATOOL ABU AKLEEN

NAHIL MOHANA

ALA'A OBAID

SONDOS SABRA

Foreword by GILLIAN SLOVO
Introduction by CARYL CHURCHILL

Edited by BASMA GHALAYINI,
JAMES HARKER & RA PAGE

BIBLIOASIS
Windsor, Ontario

First published in Great Britain in the English language by Comma Press, 2025.
First published in North America in 2025 by Biblioasis.

FIRST EDITION
2 4 6 8 10 9 7 5 3 1

Library and Archives Canada Cataloguing in Publication

Title: Voices of resistance : diaries of genocide / Batool Abu Akleen, Nahil Mohana,
Ala'a Obaid, Sondos Sabra ; foreword by Gillian Slovo ; introduction by Caryl
Churchill ; edited by Basma Ghalayini, James Harker & Ra Page.
Other titles: Voices of resistance (Biblioasis)
Names: Obaid, Ala'a, author. | Sabra, Sondos, author. | Abu Akleen, Batool, author.
Mohana, Nahil, author. | Slovo, Gillian, 1952– writer of foreword. | Churchill, Caryl,
writer of introduction. | Ghalayini, Basma, 1983– editor. | Harker, James
(Editor), editor. | Page, Ra, 1972– editor.
Identifiers: Canadiana (print) 20250247976 | Canadiana (ebook) 20250253305
ISBN 9781771967181 (softcover) | ISBN 9781771967198 (EPUB)
Subjects: LCSH: Israel-Hamas War, 2023– —Personal narratives. | LCSH: Gaza Strip—
History—Bombardment, 2023– —Personal narratives. | LCSH: Women, Palestinian
Arab—Gaza Strip—Biography. | LCSH: Palestinian Arabs—Gaza Strip—Biography.
LCSH: Women, Palestinian Arab—Gaza Strip—Social conditions.
LCSH: Palestinian Arabs—Gaza Strip—Social conditions. | LCGFT: Personal narratives.
Classification: LCC DS119.771 .V65 2025 | DDC 956.94/305509252—dc23

Prepared for the press by Daniel Wells
Cover designed by Ingrid Paulson

PRINTED AND BOUND IN CANADA

Praise for *Voices of Resistance*:

'It isn't true that there are "no words" to describe life in Gaza during the genocide. The words are here: brilliant, devastating, unexpected. Read them.'— KAMILA SHAMSIE

'An extraordinary book. *Voices of Resistance* opens a rare window into the reality of young women living under siege in the 21st century: their loss, terror and grief; their hope, ingenuity, curiosity and humour as well as despair. These testimonies come straight from hell and yet—read them, you'll see— they are radiant with undiminished life.'— OLIVIA LAING

'These diaries show us the human cost of Israel's UK-backed genocide in Gaza. When the F-35s drop their bombs, this is where they fall and this is who they fall on. Yet the writers of these diaries exhibit strength and dignity that the barbarity of colonialism can never diminish. Their love of family, of community and of the land passed down to them through generations is more enduring than all the weapons of imperialism. As these testimonies demonstrate, Gaza will survive and Palestine will be free.'— ZARAH SULTANA MP

'Heartbreaking yet illuminating, these diaries from Gaza are a must-read for all people of conscience.'— XIRAN JAY ZHAO

'*Voices of Resistance*...emerges like a siren from the wreckage. An unrelenting act of bearing witness from within annihilation. It is literature forged in real time, amid devastation.'
—ALAA ALQAISI, *The Avery Review*

'Read this book and weep, but read it also with such admiration for these four women and the community from which they come.'— REBECCA SERVADIO

Contents

★Translated by Basma Ghalayini
★★Translated by Respond Crisis Translation & Basma Ghalayini
Illustrations by Janice Hickman

FOREWORD

Gillian Slovo

WRITING ABOUT THE IMMINENT publication of her new poetry collection, Batool Abu Akleen is overcome by guilt. 'I've written all my poems on the blood of my comrades and loved ones,' she writes, 'on my pain, on my burnt fingertips, on the prospect of my own death…When I finish writing a poem…I look at it with tears welling in my eyes and heart. Oh God, how beautiful it is. And how ashamed I am that pain looks so beautiful.'

Batool's words kick off this collection, which also contains extracts from the diaries of the writers Sondos Sabra, Nahil Mohana and Ala'a Obaid. All are trapped in the Strip, forced to move countless times under unceasing bombardment. Here is beauty indeed, not least in the honesty and spirit of these four women. And horror as well. Their diaries take us to a place where the dropping off of wi-fi signal is a sign that tanks are closing in; where people have developed a whole new vocabulary for describing the sounds of different bombs; and where it becomes normal for an eight-year-old to casually ask her aunt how she would like to die.

The entries start on October 7, 2023, the day of the Hamas attack, and they end in March 2025. Eighteen months of horror, all told with such restraint, not least in Sondos Sabra's account of the murders of her niece and nephews.

And in death, life as well: we follow the pregnant Ala'a Obaid's desperate search for baby clothes and nappies, to the moment when she gives birth, alone, in a hospital bathroom. This is a place of such terrible pain, whose people know that the majority of the world either passively watches or supplies the arms and ammunition used to kill them. It is also a place where people have learned the lessons of their displaced forefathers and foremothers: no matter where you end up, you must plant seeds. And it is a place where, in an idle hour, a group of women list 25 things they hope for when the ceasefire takes hold. Number one is an end to bakery queues; number eleven is the hope that cigarettes and shisha will return, bringing a decrease in cursing; number twenty is the desire to eat grilled corn on the promenade; and then comes number twenty-five: 'I will bury my son, who remains under the rubble of my house.'

Unbearable. And yet we read these accounts knowing that people in Gaza have not only been forced to bear this, but are now facing even worse. The prospect of a ceasefire that, in 2024, provided a momentary fillip of hope to some of these accounts, was illusory. By March 2025, the Israeli blockade had created widespread famine.

Despite the oft-repeated account of the number of Israeli victims of the October 7 Hamas attack, it is not possible to fully count the Palestinians killed by the Israeli onslaught. This is not because the Hamas-run health authorities are unreliable, but because each hour brings forth more dead. At the moment of writing, the estimate stands at 54,000, not including the bodies buried under rubble.

These diaries tell us much of what it is like to live through such unending attack, but they also show us that drawing a line under any set of diaries is an arbitrary process, much like drawing a line under any point in the history of Palestine. The suffering and displacement of these women echoes the previous sufferings and displacements of their families. Nothing ends, not least their pain. And 'if our suffering no longer shocks any-one,' Ala'a Obaid writes, 'then what's the point of sharing it?'

Even in the week since I drafted this foreword, the horror has escalated. As the BBC fails to show a fact-checked film *Gaza: Medics Under Fire,* a Gazan doctor loses nine of her ten children to an Israeli bomb. As our politicians, who have done little to stop the slaughter, now demonstrate performative anger at the sheer scale of the killing, they simultaneously try to crack down on our right to protest.

Read these diaries and, no matter how much you think you already know, you will be shocked. But not only shocked: you will see the strength of these women, of their families and of their communities. Love and friendship and honesty are the threads that bind these accounts together. Read their words and weep, but read them also with such admiration for these four women and the community from which they come, and a sense of shame about how little we in the West, and our govern-ments, have done to stop this slaughter.

May 25, 2025

INTRODUCTION

Caryl Churchill

WE ALL KNOW WHAT'S happening in Gaza. Or we know something of it. Some people may not have thought about it before and imagine the trouble started when Hamas broke into Israel in October 2023. Others know more of the history of Palestine including, in relatively modern times, the British Empire, Zionism, the Nakba, the founding of Israel and the oppression and occupation that have gone on for 77 years.

But what very few of us know is what it's like to be in Gaza. Though we can see it on our screens, we can't go there. For many years it's been almost impossible to visit friends or simply visit the place, like any other place, and almost impossible to leave what has effectively become a large prison. After October 2023, what we saw on our screens was heavily weighted towards the Israeli families who'd had hostages taken. Their characters and suffering were individualised while, as more and more Palestinians were being killed, Gazan sufferings were often just reported as numbers. We could learn more from Al Jazeera and sometimes from Channel 4. Even the BBC has recently begun to show what is happening, as people have become more and more incredulous and appalled.

But with any long catastrophe, there's a danger that those of us outside of it become numbed, or distracted by the ins and outs of our own lives. Whether it's a war, an earthquake, or a famine, the watcher can begin to feel — however much they know it's not true — that the suffering people are *those* suffering people; that it's somehow not the same as if the bomb had fallen in our own street, or our own children had no water to drink. But for these four women the ins and outs of their lives are suddenly astonishingly changed and we can see and feel that.

History, of course, is often the victors' story. Israel wants that story to be theirs and is quick to try to suppress others. In 2024, Comma, the publisher of this book, took a show of Palestinian readings to HOME arts centre in Manchester — it was cancelled because of Zionist protests then reinstated because of local support. It went to Edinburgh and then to the Barbican, where extracts from some of these diaries were added, and where UK Lawyers for Israel labelled it 'illegal'. Though so much else was happening to them, these readings meant something important to the writers: their voices were being heard.

Here is what it's like to leave your home and leave again and again, be parted from your family, have a bomb fall next door, shells burst through the window, a tank attack you, lose your friend, lose children. And how ordinary things keep on at the same time, anxiety about an exam while under bombardment, and here, ordinary things change: sharing a bathroom with 30 people, queuing hours for bread, looking all day for an egg for a birthday cake, climbing over rubble as you walk down the street. Here are so many loves: for a strong father aged by war, a four-year-old sister helping make dough, a daughter playing games on a phone, a younger brother who likes to wear white and is seized and tortured, a childhood friend to laugh with, so many in each family. Here is food: the biscuit that crumbles like snow and later the food shortage, the boredom of peas. Here is a cat carried in a bag and the fat cats who have fed on rubbish and human corpses. And here is constant death: the big young man whose shroud holds remains as small as a baby's, the nephew deaf in one ear who liked watching anime, the baby whose first tooth had just come through, the child who died as she slept and her mother's wail: 'I wish I hadn't put her to bed early.'

Here is a birth and what that's like when hospitals can hardly function, the baby falling on his head but unharmed, the death of the friend who brought baby clothes a few days earlier. Here are jokes about the things Gazans now hold records for, and the noises made by different weapons, and the seller of cigarettes: one for six, two for fifteen. Here are memories of what it was like before and a determination that one day ordinary life can be lived again.

Batool's diary is the shortest and heartbreakingly ends with the joy of the January 24 ceasefire and anguish at how hard it will be to go forward. With Sondos and Nahil, we see the relief of the ceasefire and the exhaustion and grief when Israel breaks the truce and the bombing starts again. We know what the diaries don't reach: how much worse things will get. As I'm writing, in May 2025, there are more deaths every day, terrible hunger, talk of a takeover by Israel, talk of a truce, talk of Gazans forced to live somewhere else, and increasing outrage round the world, though our government shamefully supports Israel while saying it would like peace. The four diarists, I'm told, are alive.

Batool, Sondos, Nahil and Ala'a, thank you for letting me and others read your diaries, thank you for managing to write while so much was happening. Does it seem ridiculous to say your diaries are enjoyable? They're painful and make us angry but it's still a pleasure to know something of your lives. And your history.

May 16, 2025

Batool Abu Akleen

BATOOL ABU AKLEEN is a twenty-year-old Palestinian poet and translator, born and raised in Gaza City. She is a student of English Literature and Translation at the Islamic University of Gaza. At the age of fifteen, Abu Akleen won the *Parjeel Poetry Prize* for her poem 'I Did Not Steal the Cloud', which was also translated and published as part of the anthology *Di acqua e di tempo*. Her poem 'I Want a Grave' was published in Penguin's *Letters from Gaza* (2025). She was the 2024 Poet-in-Residence with Modern Poetry in Translation, for whom she collected and translated *Sea Shells: An Anthology of Emerging Poets from Gaza* (edited by Cristina Viti). Her poem 'Gunpowder' was among the winners of *The London Magazine* Poetry Prize 2025. Her debut bilingual poetry collection *48Kg* was published by Tenement Press in June 2025. Extracts from her diaries have been performed by Leila Herandi at the Belgrade Theatre, Coventry.

To Walaa, Saeed and Naria:
the light in the darkness,
the laughter in the midst of death.

MORNINGS ARE WORRISOME AND PAINFUL

I, THE CREATURE WHO once loved mornings the most, can no longer tolerate them.

I wake up trembling. Something in my heart feels wrong, like everything else around me. I wrap my head in three blankets, making sure my ears are covered, but before I can even hear myself breathe, the epic morning noise begins. From beyond the blankets: the sound of my younger siblings, quarrelling over half a piece of pita bread.

My mother begins to rebuke them, 'You want to embarrass us in the eyes of the neighbours? Everyone's flour is running out, you're the only ones shouting about it.'

My head is filled with the desire to leave: to escape this cosmic hell by any means necessary, even if leaving means death. My body is tied down, my joints knotted by fear. I remember my grandmother, who used to relieve my fear after every Israeli aggression with a little olive oil and many prayers. Today, my joints are bound tighter than ever, and my grandmother is not here to comfort me.

The funniest thing of all, and I don't know if it's really funny, is that the fear I'm experiencing isn't a fear of death or annihilation, but rather a fear of life. It's a fear of the Phonetics exam I'm taking in the coming days, of my haphazard Italian learning, of my inability to complete anything, of missing opportunities, of falling behind my classmates at university, of the possibility of gaining or losing weight.

Death has never frightened me; it has only restricted me, casting black, petrified sadness on my heart. But this morning my fear of life grows and grows, and with it a great anger at my inability to overcome fear. I cry under the covers and wish for the return of my grandmother with her tin of olive oil.

We are displaced: my mother, myself and my four younger siblings (Hadi, Taqwa, Raghad and Maryam), living in a tent in Deir al-Balah, in the centre of the Gaza Strip. This four-by-four-metre room serves as our living area, bedroom, study and work space. Behind a small partition is our kitchen and dining area: two-metres-by-four. Our tent is made of leather with an iron frame and waterproof triangular roof. By this measure, we might be considered aristocratic among the displaced.

My mother is making tea. I no longer get angry about my family waking up at six o'clock, disrupting the only hour of the day when I might have found some peace. While still under the covers, I begin to read from my phone, as I do every morning: the one habit my knotted joints haven't hindered. My mother places a cup of tea next to my head and brings me ghorayeba [a type of shortbread made from flour, sugar and ghee]. Today is my sister Maryam's ninth birthday, her second during this genocide. My mother has baked ghorayeba to celebrate.

When Maryam turned eight, she cried every day, asking, 'Where's Dad?' Recently she's started to say, 'I want to see my grandmother. Why did they kill her?'

In my entire life, I've never loved any biscuit more than ghorayeba. I've always identified with it. In Arabic, its pronunciation is a variation on the word 'strange'. Its texture is so hard that, as soon as you take the first bite, the rest of the biscuit begins to crumble all over your clothes like white snow. It's fragile like negotiations, pretends to be tough like I do every day and melts in your mouth just like my toughness melts when I notice the buzzing of Israeli drones above our heads. Ghorayeba can only be eaten once it's cold. Cold like this tent.

My mother sits beside me, watching, and hoping her ghor-ayeba will alleviate the depression that's been eating me up for days. I have no idea how to deal with this depression, or how to dampen its severity even a little. So I retreat again under the blankets and continue reading on my phone.

Before ten minutes have passed, little Rania—or as I like to call her, 'Naria' [meaning: firey]—enters our tent, followed by her mother, Walaa. Naria is four years old. Walaa is 24, just a few years older than me. Walaa's family comes from al-Majdal [in Historic Palestine]. Her grandparents were displaced to Jabalia, north of Gaza City, where she grew up as a refugee. After getting married, she moved to the Sheikh Radwan neighbourhood, before the Israeli's displaced her here along with her husband Saeed and his family. Walaa's parents and siblings remain in the North, divided—like me from my father—by distance and by this genocide. Walaa and her family live in the tent next to ours. But as our relationship has grown stronger, our families have spent more and more time together sharing food, drink, sadness and joy. Sometimes, Walaa even spends the night with us.

With eight people in one tent, the noise grows louder, soon matched by noise from the surrounding tents. Close to 900 people live around us in this camp. *Oh God, how I hate these sounds!* By now, the option of getting up has become a must. So I get up. My limbs are still knotted as I tidy my blankets and go to wash my face and brush my teeth. But recently—and by 'recently', I mean, 'for the last year and a few months'—I've been having memory problems. As soon as I reach the small wash-hut beside our tent, I realise I've forgotten my toothbrush and have to go back to retrieve it from the empty pea tin I've set aside for pens and other random things.

The wash-hut is our own construction: built from old pieces of wood and blankets left behind by our former neighbours in the displacement camp in Rafah, before they returned to their

5

homes in al-Qarara (which had not yet been bombed) and we resumed our displacement journey here, to Deir al-Balah. The hut stands beside our tent, and contains a 250 litre water barrel and a stove, which we use for cooking during gas shortages. In our tent, the ground is covered by a kind of plastic rug. Here in the hut, the soil is exposed.

I pour away the murky water that's collected in the bowl under the barrel's plastic tap, refill it and begin to wash my face. The water is salty and cold, it jolts me into alertness, much like a bullet. Perhaps my depression is due to the fact that I couldn't sleep till after midnight last night and woke up at 5am. I love little Naria, but today in particular, I don't want to see her. I don't want any more noise.

I say to myself, 'Why not try one of those techniques psychologists always claim will improve your mood?'

I attempt some cardio exercises, copied from a YouTube video. I really don't remember the last time I tried something like this. After ten minutes, I no longer feel depressed: my mental pain has been overpowered by the physical pain of stiff limbs from sleeping on the barren dirt.

I prepare to wash my body, heating water on the stove because the baker, Umm Khalil, who usually heats water for us, is busy preparing trays of chicken. Chicken has been absent from the market for months; we thought we would never see it again. My family will have to wait another week until prices drop a little, but the smell drums on the wall of my stomach as soon as it enters my nose.

I pour the heated water into a tattered blue plastic bucket, which only has a couple of months left in it, and top it up with some cold water from the tap. I place my winter clothes in an empty UNRWA food carton along with some shampoo, a bottle of conditioner my mother purchased by mistake and the empty tin of peas which I'll use to scoop water from the bucket. All of this I carry to a small bathroom, which is made of zinc sheets and adjoined to three other bathrooms with such little privacy you can hear the other users breathing. I hang my clothes on the nails that Saeed has hammered into the zinc, and shower myself with the pea tin, listening to the neighbours' children arguing over who should take the next wash.

Each bathroom in the camp is shared by at least three families, sometimes four. The average size of a family in the camp is six, meaning most bathrooms are shared by at least eighteen people. I am lucky, only having to share this room with a maximum of eleven people.

As I bathe, I notice my hair has grown down to a little below the middle of my back. I want to say it has grown quickly, but then I remember that fifteen months of this genocide have passed. My hair is also falling out at an alarming rate; I don't know how to stop it.

After washing, I return to the tent and read a few pages of Al-Hamadhani's *Maqamat*,[1] borrowed from the only library I can find in Deir al-Balah. Then, I remember my exams are a few days away and I try to revise. I am studying for a degree in English Literature, with a minor in Translation, at the Islamic University of Gaza, and this is my second year.

At the start of the genocide, the Islamic University was destroyed by Israeli forces. A few weeks later, on December 6, 2023, my beloved professor Refaat Alareer[2] was murdered in a targeted Israeli bombing, which also killed his brother, his sister and four of his nephews. Six or seven months after the genocide started, our studies resumed online.

Children are milling around me. My mother is trying to bake a birthday cake for Maryam. I put on my Bluetooth headphones, which work in one ear and not the other, and set a Phonetics lecture to run at double speed because my laptop battery only lasts an hour and a half. After 30 minutes of loading and reloading the lecture with crappy internet connection, I haven't learnt a thing.

I'm relapsing again. My anxiety has returned, worse than this morning. I try wrapping my head in the blankets, but nothing stops the feeling this time. *Oh God, how it hurts*: my lungs threatening to burst through my rib cage, my heart exploding in my chest, my whole body in knots. I call out to my mother, desperately wanting her to recite some prayers and ruqyahs[3] over me. But she is crying too; my neighbour Walaa and my sisters are trying to soothe her.

I'm not even able to ask what's wrong. I can't leave my mattress. It's as if this mattress is a prison cell. The noise of the camp is suffocating me.

My body doesn't relax until everyone is asleep. Now, in the dead of night, the only real noise comes from the maternity centre affiliated with al-Awda Hospital. And there's another sound, too, echoing inside my head, like the flatline on a heart rate monitor.

January 12, 2025

EACH PERSON'S PAIN IS THEIRS ALONE

'Town centre, town centre, town centre!'

The voices of cart and tuk-tuk drivers ring out in the street. But there are no calls from taxi drivers and no taxis in sight. This change in transportation — the widespread disappearance of taxis — still surprises me, even after more than a year. Before the genocide, I used to choose my ride based on trivial things: this car doesn't have air conditioning; that driver looks suspicious; this car's empty and I'm afraid to ride alone; that car's back seat is full of men and I don't want to sit next to them. All these options used to pass by in two minutes or less.

These days, I choose between a horse and a tuk-tuk, if I can find a tuk-tuk. Otherwise, I choose between a horse and a donkey. If I'm lucky, I'll find my ride in ten minutes. If God and all his angels are pleased with, or pity me, I'll find the impossible: a car.

Today, I'm in a hurry, meaning luck frowns on me and I'm forced to stand for half an hour, cursing and swearing at everything, wishing for the death of the donkeys, the horses, the drivers and the occupation. Alongside these wishes, I wish for the disappearance of this homeland itself—a place that confuses the entire world—so that all of us can go to a place where there is no fatigue or hardship; so that no one else will have to be born in a place as sad as this.

Tears well in my eyes as a couple of donkey carts arrive. To preserve my privilege of choice, I choose the slightly faster donkey: driven by a man, not a child.

If something happens, I'll be able to hold the driver accountable, I think. And then I laugh at myself for believing that law still exists, that someone will protect me if things go wrong.

I climb into the cart and sit cross-legged, in all my elegance, with my hand on my cheek and head lowered, scorched by the midday sun.

The woman sitting next to me asks, 'Where are you from? You look displaced.'

Like a robot, programmed to answer, I reply, 'Yes, I'm from Gaza City.'

'Where in Gaza City?'

'From Rimal, Auntie. Do you know that street with the post office, the one near the Shawa and Hoasri Tower, that leads to Taj Mall? I used to live there.'

'Yes, by God,' she replies. 'We're from al-Zaytoun.'

Her words flash through my mind. I remember my grandmother, Safa; our Eid visits to the family home; the watermelons my cousin Fawzi would spend all day cutting till the pieces were exactly equal in size.

In the silence that grows between me and my fellow passenger, I drift back to the last days spent in my home, when I would hear the sound of ambulances all day long, speeding like lightning across al-Wahda Street to al-Shifa Medical Complex;

9

when I would watch the reporters in the Shawa and Hosari Tower [home to many press organisations] from the living room window, while my father watched them on TV. I would see them all from that window, and their presence comforted me. But the number of lit windows in the Shawa and Hosari Tower diminished day by day, until they all went out and their sound died down. Only Wael al-Dahdouh remained.[4] I watched him closely until he too left.

After that, I looked into my mother's eyes and said, 'Mum, even Wael is gone. If something happens to us, there's no one around: no ambulance, no hospital, no communications, not even Wael. Now Wael's left, what are we doing here?'

My memories are interrupted by the voice of my fellow passenger: 'Did your house collapse or is it still standing?'

'They tore the tower apart like a cake,' I answer. 'It collapsed on the third day of Ramadan.'

'May God compensate you with something better. And where are you staying now?'

'In a tent.'

The conversation doesn't last much longer, I've become accustomed to this. The unbearable traffic has transformed shared rides into daily funerals in which each passenger remembers their lost home and martyred loved ones. Everyone talks about their pain casually, nobody cries. I really don't know what prevents the sadness from appearing on our faces, or what stops our mouths from trembling as they recall all this pain. It's not because the tragedy of others makes the burden of our own tragedies lighter or less important. It seems each person's pain is theirs alone.

Haifa Street in al-Baraka area of Deir al-Balah has changed dramatically. The rubble of a bombed-out building that used to block the street has finally been removed. They'd been waiting for a ceasefire to clear things up, but it seems the genocide will never end.

Just north of al-Baraka roundabout, I decide to abandon the cart, running instead to escape the bodies that keep bumping into me, the traffic that threatens to plough over me, the smell of sweat mingled with men's cologne and the sewage that fills each street. But no matter how fast I run, the sounds are inescapable. *Oh God, these sounds are the sign of life here, but they only bring me death.*

Vendors fill the pavement. There are stalls everywhere. At the edge of the market, near the roundabout, the prices are highest. But the deeper you go, the cheaper things become. Once again, you're given the privilege of choice: you either pay more on the outskirts, or bump into more bodies and risk being trampled by a donkey in the heart of the market.

It scares me how well people adapt. It scares me that people can dress in the morning as if nothing has happened. Women put on makeup and still look their best; men carry briefcases and keep going to work. I look down at the rings on my fingers, wipe the remnants of kohl from my eyes and wonder if I, like them, have adapted.

In fifteen months of genocide, I've abandoned all my manners in the same way the world has abandoned us. I've become fierce and cruel to suit the jungle that Gaza has become. I used to be the spoiled girl who, whenever anyone spoke rudely to her, would call out to Daddy to solve her problems, or cry in Mama's lap.

Now I stand, open my mouth wide, and shout: 'You! The donkey who's driving the donkey, do you want to cut off my leg today or what? Bugger off.'

Or: 'Tell him to eat shit and stop talking on behalf of Gaza.'

Or: 'For fuck's sake, who does he think he is?'

After escaping the crowds, I arrive at a café in Abu Aref: a café I used to visit weekly. I plan to spend the day here, editing a few poems and coaxing out others which are still stuck in my head.

It is exactly 10am in the morning. The café is full of citrus, palm and olive trees. No one but me visits the café at such an early hour. I sit on a chair, resting my back.

Silence…silence…silence…

Balance returns and I come back to myself. Suddenly, I am overcome by an intense desire to sleep, as if this renewed sense of calm is whispering in my head, 'It's OK, it's OK, just close your eyes.'

January 14, 2025

ALL THIS PAIN ASSESSING IS RIDICULOUS

The day before yesterday, Real Madrid played Barcelona. Back then, the latest ceasefire negotiations were still in their infancy and no one paid attention. Young people watched the match passionately, and at night, when the city was blackly silent, their cheers filled the streets. The euphoria of victory and the disappointment of loss prevailed.

Yesterday, as rumours of progress in the negotiations grew, my mother and our neighbour, Walaa, discussed our return to the North—what they would take, what they would wear, how we would return. My mother said that a tuk-tuk would be enough to transport Walaa, Naria, Saeed and their few belongings home. Whereas we would need a lorry to transport ours. She told Walaa about the house my father has rented for us and how, when we return, we won't have to live in a tent any more.

Today, I sip my morning coffee, a small cup ordered from the same man who yesterday complained that I made one coffee last all day. I don't know why I didn't tell him, 'What business is it of yours? If you don't like me ordering just one coffee, find me a job with a good salary and I promise I'll order more.'

The rumoured breakthrough in the ceasefire negotiations causes me to sip with greater fear today—not fear of disappointment should the negotiations fall through—but fear of truly accepting that our house and everything in it has been destroyed; that my grandmother and my friends have been killed and won't come back; of returning to my city, whose beauty has become a pile of ashes; of seeing my father for the first time in more than a year.

And how is my father? For ten years, he tried to lose a single kilogram, without success. Now, he has lost twenty kilograms in a few months. In pictures, he reminds me of myself. Every time I look in the mirror, I realise I share more of his features.

How will you greet us, Dad? How will I react, when I see you again?

Everyone I've spoken to today has said, 'May you return to your father soon, inshallah. May God reunite you in peace.'

In moments of heightened anticipation, emotions pour out of me in ways I don't expect. Waiting for the publisher to announce my poetry collection last month, I burst into tears for two hours because my father wasn't by my side, and because I couldn't hug my friends Rawan and Maryam. I remember the guilt that overcame me because I'd written all my poems on the blood of my comrades and loved ones, on my pain, on my burnt fingertips, on the prospect of my own death. Poems built from death can never bring pride; they can only bring more pain. My poetry is nothing but stylised pain. When I finish writing a poem and it seems perfectly crafted, I look at it with tears welling in my eyes and heart. *Oh God, how beautiful it is. And how ashamed I am that pain looks so beautiful.*

I'm sitting at a table among the olive trees. Whenever I raise my head, their branches meet my gaze. I'm trying to work on a digital pamphlet for *MPT* [*Modern Poetry in Translation*]: a collection of Gazan poets and poetry.[5] But how do I find the capacity to evaluate the beauty and ugliness of my own poems, let alone edit others' poems written about their personal pain during this genocide? How have I dared to reject some of these poets because their poems aren't good enough? Who am I to tell someone being subjected to genocide that their pain isn't well crafted, that their pain doesn't seem authentic, that their pain isn't painful enough?

This is ridiculous. All of this pain assessing is ridiculous.

I feel like I'm sitting on the edge of hell. My feet keep moving and so does my head. I'm doing nothing but trying to distract myself. I look up and see my mother and my sister Taqwa waving to me among the olive branches. They join me at the table, telling me they are on their way to the market in search of some vitamins and medicine after the doctor informed them of Taqwa's blood test results, which were not at all promising. Anticipation of a ceasefire hangs over all of us. I pack away my poetry and open Al Jazeera on my phone, cursing the café owner and his weak internet connection; cursing the world and all its mediators, parties and negotiators.

Back in the tent, I lie on my mattress. Fear and anxiety gnaw at me and I do nothing but surrender to them, falling asleep, or rather just closing my eyes. My body is so exhausted I can't move. I stay like this, listening to the sounds around me: the songs from the party our neighbour Modi has thrown for his wedding, the applause of his campmates, the pounding of airstrikes, the buzzing of drones.

After three hours, I muster up the courage to check the news again and I'm shocked to still be receiving work emails on my phone. Here I am, on the edge of death or life; can no one honour this moment with some quiet? Then I burst into tears, scared that our hope is nothing but a lie. My mother hugs me and tries to calm me down. I cry even more.

My sister Taqwa says, 'It's OK, nothing's wrong with you.'

My brother Hadi says: 'What are you crying about? It can't get any worse.'

I pull the blankets over my head and watch the news broadcasts on my phone. Notifications ping from my coursemates on

WhatsApp: wishes for the genocide to stop, complaints about the shortness of the exam period, arguments over a proposal to postpone the exams if people are allowed to return to the North.

Walaa and my sisters prepare a pot of coffee and a tray of Halab fingers [sweet pastries] — enough for the entire camp — to celebrate the truce that hasn't yet been announced. Wrapped in my blankets, I walk like a mummy to Walaa's tent, where we devour the entire tray.

Then we wait, and we wait, and we wait…

The sound of the wedding party fills the air, now mixed with a chant of 'Truce! Truce! Truce!', as if the whole camp is trying to summon the truce towards us, to force it to come.

It's a tradition, on the last day of an aggression, for the Israeli warplanes to go crazy and carry out as many airstrikes as possible, as if they're racing to use every missile. After the 2021 aggression, my grandmother called to tell us that her neighbour had been martyred just five minutes before the ceasefire went into effect. It seems ridiculous to me: surviving all that, then dying at the last minute.

January 15, 2025

THE TRUCE IS ANNOUNCED

Today, I've thrown aside my poems and done nothing except watch the live news on Al Jazeera, waiting for Qatar to announce a ceasefire, and terrified the broadcaster will say, 'End of negotiations. The war continues.'[6]

I sit with Walaa, Saeed and Naria, covering myself with their blankets.

After a few hours, Walaa decides to make us a pot of sahlab [a sweet milky drink]. I love it when Walaa makes sweets; she's very generous with the sugar. I help by preparing a mixture of

15

sugar, cinnamon and roasted peanuts, which my sister Taqwa accidentally burns.

The pot leaks onto the stove. My mother looks at it and says, 'No problem, once we get home, we'll get a new one.'

Suddenly, Walaa shouts, 'Saeed, Saeed! Raise the phone so we can all see!'

On the tiny phone screen, the Qatari commissioner stands up and announces: 'The agreement has been signed, the ceasefire will be implemented as soon as Sunday at exactly twelve-thirty AM.'

My body trembles and I laugh.

I leave the tent and my ears are flooded with noise they can finally delight in: the joy in the street; ululations; bullets fired in celebration, their sound and light breaking the darkness. My heart, shattered since the first ceasefire deal failed, can barely believe this moment.

I think: *I'll change the biographies of the Gazan poets I've collected for the poetry magazine; I'll write next to their names: 'Survivors of the genocide!'*

I used to say: 'Everything has an end. The genocide has an end and I have an end. And I don't know which will end before the other.' In truth, I never expected to outlive this genocide. I never expected to triumph over death without a scratch on my body, without even losing a limb.

We used to say that we wouldn't rejoice when the genocide ended in honour of our lost loved ones. We used to say that we wouldn't rejoice because our true tragedy would come to light. We used to say that, when we were no longer busy trying to escape death, we would devote ourselves to seeing what it had taken from us.

But I don't feel any of this, I only feel joy. I have seen the truth of the human spirit: individualism overwhelms everything and is difficult to contain. The fear of sharing one's home, one's clothes, and most importantly, one's food. The desire to own everything because you fear it will run out. The intense struggle with your soul to share food while the fear of starving consumes you. The fear and the anger: the fear of hunger, and the anger at feeling your survival is more important than others'.

When a missile falls and you hear its sound, you smile. You smile because you are still alive, even though you know that another person was killed the very moment you realised you were safe. You pray for the one who was killed and you grieve, but your joy is greater than all of this: your joy that you didn't die and that no one you loved died. You rejoice while others grieve. You rejoice when you realise that the home that was bombed wasn't yours, but the one right behind it. You feel a little sad, but you're still happy about your survival. Survival is individual, always individual. Joy is individual, and so is grief.

When Dr Refaat was killed, the news reached me in the middle of the night. Everyone was asleep, and I was curled up in the middle of our old house, on the floor, grieving. When my family woke up the next day, they ridiculed my grief. I was indignant that no one understood or sympathised with what I felt. But grief is individual.

You continue to grieve while the world goes on with its life. Your neighbours laugh, and you sit alone with your pain. No matter how hard we try to portray ourselves as one people, no matter how united we are, individualism will always prevail. It's as if this body separates you from others, as if this mould that frames your soul, in reality, isolates it. All the concepts and representations that make us appear unified are false.

When I watched the Qatari commissioner announcing the ceasefire, I didn't think about Dr Refaat or my grandmother Safa, or Tamer, or Nada, or Bilal, or Raghad, or Abu Sami, or anyone. I didn't think about the home I'd lost. I only thought about the fact that I'd survived. I laughed and began to imagine my future. *Am I afraid to admit my loss?* After the genocide is over,

I won't mention the names of any of those I've lost. I won't visit their graves. I won't go to the street where my house used to be. I don't want to see its rubble.

I don't want to remember any of this.

I sit alone, listening to the ululations and reading the news. My body starts to accept that it will not have to resist again, I begin to feel bruises on every part of it. And I burst into tears because this will end.

It will end.

January 16, 2025

DON'T LET ME DIE AFRAID

6:54pm

I have about two days left before I can call myself a 'survivor'. Just two more days and this will all be over, if I manage to survive this barrage of airstrikes.

I feel so angry that I'm studying now instead of spending time imagining the life that awaits me, a life in which death will no longer stand by and whistle in my ear. I put on my headphones, listen to random songs chosen by SoundCloud and try to focus. The sound of bombs and drones overwhelms the music. *What if I'm killed at this very moment, in the final hours of this genocide?* I keep imagining the missile that will land on my head and destroy me. Then, I smile: *at least I'll die knowing the genocide is almost over.* I slap my face and try to go back to studying.

But really, what if I don't survive?

8:57pm

I almost got killed.

I've always wondered if God has given me a seventh vision: if these ghosts, prophecies and images expressed through my pen are unhappy warnings of the future. I've never imagined misery without it coming to pass. In 'I Didn't Steal the Cloud', a poem I wrote when I was fifteen, I imagined myself wandering the alleys of the refugee camps and living in them.

And here I am, living in a camp.

In 'Cemetery', the poem I wrote today, I imagined this camp would become a cemetery, and this white tent a shroud. My seventh vision couldn't miss the feeling that a missile would fall on me and crush me as I held this blue pen?

And the missile did fall, but it didn't crush my body; it crushed my soul with fear. I had gone to the bathroom — an act that always scares me at night — and above the tents I saw the plane, saw its red light illuminating the sky. I fell to the ground, curled up reciting the Shahada,[7] closed my eyes, squeezed them until they were about to explode, and waited...waited to die.

So it turns out I wasn't going to burn happy in the knowledge that a truce will come. I was going to burn while I was afraid.

Oh God, please don't let me die afraid.

January 17, 2025

I'VE CURSED MY LUCK FOR BEING A WOMAN

Throughout the night, I was plagued by dreams of bombing. Some were beautiful because I was with my father. We were at home, sitting together with my mother, and the missiles were falling with a sound so loud. But I wasn't afraid. I wasn't afraid because I was in my father's arms.

Today, Samira, who was our neighbour before her brother kicked her out, visits us. She's an example of the woman I want to be. She has a car and a job with a stable monthly salary. She has never needed anyone in her entire life. But during a genocide, sometimes even money won't help you find shelter.

Samira sits and talks with us for a long time. We discover that our suffering is the same. When you are a woman alone, the

19

world sees you as air, or perhaps worse, as a miserable creature with broken wings, in need of protection. Perhaps this would be different if we were women in a time other than genocide, supported by a higher authority in society: a police force and the rule of law.

I don't know.

I don't know if a law can make any difference in this world. International law was unable to protect me from being called a human animal[8] and seeing the remains of men, women and children being scraped up into blue plastic bags.[9] I truly don't think there is any point in human laws.

When you're a woman alone, no matter how peaceful you are, no matter how hard you try to keep yourself to yourself, that person will always appear and call you a whore, insult you, convince everyone to talk badly about you. You will always be looked at: 'Look at how she walks. Look how she talks. Look how she dresses and how she always appears. She doesn't have a man to control her.'

At moments such as these, I wish my father was by my side. None of them would dare to open their mouths.

My mother has tried to console me: 'Batool, my dear, we are not in our own city and the world is not peaceful.'

But there have been many times when I've cursed my luck for being born a woman, with such a stigma attached to myself. If I hadn't been a woman, none of them would have insulted me. I would have been free to decide when I went out and when I came back to the tent. A crazy woman wouldn't have threatened to kill me, loudly and in public, because she thought the young man she wanted her daughter to marry liked me instead. At least, she wouldn't have done it without anyone holding her accountable.

If I hadn't been a woman, I wouldn't have had to worry when the sanitary pads ran out in the market. I wouldn't have become angry at my own body, which conspired against me by giving me two periods in one month. I wouldn't have thought about the effects of genocide on my oestrogen and progesterone levels, my skin and my body.

A woman has to think about all of these things.

Dear Shams,

I realise I haven't given you a name. I realise I've stopped naming my notebooks and I don't know why. Perhaps because, after fifteen months of genocide, everything seems nameless. All my attempts to understand what I've felt and what has happened around me have proven futile. Perhaps that's why I've stopped naming everything.

Today, I was reading an old diary—in a notebook named 'Milad'—and my body began to tremble. This entire year, which I had been trying to forget and deny, was brought back to me in just a few pages.

On February 3, 2024, almost a year ago, I'd recorded Al Jazeera's announcement that a ceasefire agreement had been reached and agreed to by both Hamas and Israel. At that time, my house still existed, my grandmother hadn't been killed, Tamer hadn't been killed. At that time, hope grew within me.

Then it became clear that 'truce' was nothing more than a word poured over my hope like acid, burning it to its core. From that moment until five days ago, I stopped following the news. And what if this new truce is really just like that one? What if nothing happens? At least now I'm reassured that I won't die as soon as I discover it's a lie. I've felt that pain before, I'll be able to overcome it again

I reached the page in 'Milad' where I talked about the two-month anniversary of Dr Refaat's martyrdom. Today marks a year, a month, and six days since his murder. So much has changed, except for the gap his passing left inside me.

As I write, the smell of meat stir-fried with onions wafts from our tent and drifts through the camp. I don't feel guilty; I don't worry that someone hungry might pass by and suffer. Yesterday, they distributed coupons for one kilo of beef, one litre of sunflower oil and one kilo of sugar to most of the camp's residents, all except for a few families — the poorest and most vulnerable — who simply don't have the connections to intimidate and threaten the camp officials. When my mother went to collect our coupon, the official spoke to her with a raised nose and that pious tone, saying that he had already distributed the coupons to the satisfaction of his conscience and that he feared only God.

Before the genocide, I always hated meat. I could never stand its taste. Now I eat meat voraciously, though I still hate it. I just don't have many options.

I think my taste buds have been distorted by the genocide: the white bean dish, once my favourite meal, is now something I detest. And peas, the mere name of which used to terrify me, are something I've grown to grudgingly love. I've even started eating molokhia [jute mallow], the texture of which always bothered me. And spinach, and soup...I devour them with relish. Is this what hunger does: strips me of my right to choose and corrupts my tongue?

January 18, 2025

I REMEMBER ANNE FRANK

Dear Shams,

I'm still scared and upset, even though I dance and sing:

> *I'm returning to my country*
> *I'm returning to my country*
> *To the barren land*
> *I'm returning to my country*10

Our neighbour, Umm Hassan, says, 'I've never seen Batool so excited and happy.'

I tell her, 'I've always been like this, Umm Hassan, but the war extinguished my joy.'

I show Walaa my old photos. I ask her insistently, 'Walaa, did I look different before the genocide?'

She answers, 'Yes, your face was clear, but now it's covered in pimples. Your face was glowing, but now it's dim.'

Everyone's appearance has changed: they've lost a few kilograms, gained a few more, their faces have darkened, they've grown older. But I've remained more or less the same, and I don't really know if I'm happy about that. I want this pain to be visible; I don't want to have to explain it.

I remember my childhood: reading about great poets and writers. A common refrain in every writer's biography was: 'He survived such-and-such...He lived through such-and-such a war...He was almost killed by such-and-such...' I always imagined my future in those terms: could I become a great writer, facing death without succumbing?

My father laughed when I shared this daydream: 'Isn't "from the heart of the Gaza siege" enough of a biography for you?'

'But we're living normally. I mean, these people were facing death.'

I laugh at how seriously I took this idea. In a way, now, I have died. But does death add a special beauty to poetry? Or is it just that the terror death creates makes everything written in and about it sacred? Either way, I've gone from being the pampered daughter of a father afraid to let her go farther than Tel al-Hawa [a neighbourhood in Gaza City], to a woman fending for herself with a broken heart. Tomorrow the genocide will end. And ten days after that, I will turn twenty.

Food prices are starting to return to normal. I still can't believe it. (I'm crying as I write these words.) Tonight, I will sleep for the last time while we are being exterminated. Just a few hours left to endure before we can start over. When I return home—I mean to the North, for we no longer have a home—I want to close my eyes the whole way. I want to go blind, to embrace my father without sight. I want to tell myself: my grandmother is still here, but I don't have time to visit her. Dr. Refaat is running late for his classes, so I won't see him on the steps of Building N. The university is still here, I'm just too tired to go today. My body aches because I'm sick, not from sadness. This house I'm staying in is just a temporary place while my father paints our home. My belongings are still there, and so are my clothes, but I'm tired, so I won't bring them now. And Huda...Huda is still here. We just had a small disagreement so I won't visit her today, but I still love her, and I'll see her again soon. In fact: they're all waiting for me. I'm just tired, a little tired, so I've postponed their visits for another day.

Today, I had the final exam for the second year of my English Literature degree. The internet in the camp had stopped working, so I went to the café, despite my mother's objections. All the way, I thought about the possibility of being killed alone in the café, or returning to the camp to find my entire family murdered. I realised this was one of the last times I'd walk these streets. I wore a pistacchio-coloured hijab which clashed with my old brown sweatshirt. I reviewed the final notes for my exam while listening to the voices of the other patrons: 'Come on, man. Tomorrow, I will kiss your soil, Shuja'iyya.'

I thought of Dr Refaat, and slapped myself because I didn't have time to remember anything but the exam material.

Today, for the first time, the pea tekkeya[11] was open and we didn't rush to get a pot. Today, for the first time, we all admitted how much we hate peas. My mother suggested falafel, and for the first time since we moved to Deir al-Balah, I helped her prepare falafel with chickpeas, not with dried peas or yellow lentils. I remember the time we tried making falafel with yellow lentils and how nauseating the taste was. It was so hard, it challenged the strength of our teeth.

We prepared a salad plate that would have cost 100 shekels a month ago: fried aubergine and chips, saj bread, red peppers, tomato sauce, tahini with parsley and a pot of extremely sweet tea. All of this was a dream. And now I've eaten it, I'm not hungry. I won't be hungry again.

As we ate, I looked into the eyes of Walaa, Saeed and Ranoush and told them, 'This is one of our last lunches together.'

I am planning to surprise Rawan when I return. She's been my best friend for seven years. Her home, unlike ours, hasn't been destroyed by the genocide.

I am still afraid of being killed at the last minute, still afraid that one of my friends will be killed at the last minute. Nour and I were discussing our exam, and I told her, 'Nour, we're going to survive, right? We're not going to die at the last minute. We don't have to die at the last minute. Nour, don't die.'

I remember Anne Frank, whose diary I finished reading a few days before October 7. Anne didn't survive, but I did...I mean, I have a few hours left to survive.

I send a revised Arabic version of my first collection of poems to my friend Ruby, in London, so she can publish it if I am killed tonight. Then I provide my editor, Luna, with the email addresses of the poets whose work I have been compiling. If I die, I don't want anything left unfinished.

January 19, 2025

THE FIRST MORNING OF THE CEASEFIRE

My dear Shams,

At the first white light of day, I dressed as if it were Eid and waited for 8:30am. Time seemed to have stopped and stuck at 7:30. I expected to cry, but there was nothing but the stupid smile I fall into when I'm very happy. The ceasefire is supposed to have begun, but the planes are still hovering overhead, still bombing and killing. Yes, the planes are bombing and joy is pumping through my veins, no airstrike can stop it.

I repeat, 'Truce, truce.'

Everyone keeps saying it.

I want to believe it. And even if it's another lie, I'll pretend I haven't realised yet. All I want is to sleep. I don't know how I'll take my Translation exam in a few hours.

Dear Shams,

The genocide is over. I'm writing to you at 10:20pm, after the first day of the ceasefire has passed. I can't deny how happy I am.

In the morning, after we hugged each other and said, 'We're going home, we're going home,' I remembered that I had no home. *Where are my clothes? Where is my house? Where are my old diaries and notebooks? Where is the warm bathroom I'm waiting to use?*

I dozed for an hour, just as I'd hoped to do when the truce began, then quickly got ready to go to the café and take my exam. The road was the same as it has been every day: still filled with sewage, displaced people's tents, ridiculous stalls, gloomy faces.

Is that all?

Will no one wipe away the city's bleak face?

I arrived at the café. 'An internet card, please, and a heavy cup of coffee.'

Heavy, like my heavy, heavy head.

I drank the coffee and ate Abu al-Walad biscuits [custard creams], which tasted like babies' cereal. I kept staring at the faces around me: the same faces that populate the café every day. None of them had taken a day off; today was the same as every other day. I reluctantly reviewed some notes, thinking about everything, about the Islamic University, which will return to how it was when it was first founded: tents and static caravans.

I finished the exam and returned to the camp.

But why is there still a camp? Why hasn't everything that was lost been restored? Why hasn't Gaza returned?

NOTES

1. Al-Hamadhani's *Maqamat:* A ninth-century collection of prose and poetry which follows the picaresque adventures of a witty protagonist.

2. Dr Refaat Alareer: Poet, educator and activist. Dr Refaat's poem 'If I Must Die', written just weeks before his assassination in the Israeli airstrike described by Batool, has become a symbol of Palestinian resilience and resistance. Drawing on a tradition which includes Emily Dickinson's 'If I Should Die', Claude McKay's 'If We Should Die', and Rupert Brooke's 'The Soldier', Dr Refaat's now-famous poem opens with the lines: If I must die, / you must live / to tell my story.'

3. Ruqyahs: Specific verses from *The Quran*, believed to target certain ailments.

4. Wael al-Dahdouh: Prominent journalist. Al-Dahdouh's wife, son, daughter and grandson were killed by an Israeli airstrike on October 25, 2023. Al-Dahdouh was subsequently injured in an Israeli drone strike on a Gazan school on December 15, 2023, during which his colleague (Al Jazeera cameraman Samer Abu Daqqa) was murdered. On January 7, 2024, al-Dahdouh's eldest son, journalist Hamza al-Dahdouh, was assassinated alongside two colleagues in an Israeli missile strike targeting his press vehicle.

5. This pamphlet was later published by MPT as *Sea Shells: An Anthology of Emerging Poets from Gaza.*

6. 'End of negotiations. The war continues'. This is a line from Batool's poem 'End of War', which appears in her collection *48Kg*, published by Tenement Press.

7. Shahada: The Islamic declaration of faith: 'There is no God but God and Muhammad is his messenger'.

8. Yoav Gallant, then Israeli Defense Minister, referred to Gazans as 'human animals' while announcing a complete siege on the Strip on October 9, 2023.

9. Due to the extreme violence and intensity of Israeli airstrikes, and their effects on human bodies, many Gazans have been forced to collect the remains of their loved ones in plastic bags, as reported by *Haaretz* and Al Jazeera.

10. Batool is singing the revolutionary folk song '*Raja'e a Beladi*' [I'm Returning to my Country]. Batool changes the traditional lyrics, substituting 'green land' with 'barren land'.

11. Tekkeya: A community food station which offers dishes free of charge.

Sondos Sabra

SONDOS SABRA, 25, holds a bachelor's degree in English Literature from the Islamic University of Gaza and is a founding member of the Shaghaf Youth Initiative, which organises discussions of literary works. She is a translator and writer. Her writing has appeared in *Mondoweiss*, *The New Statesman* and *ArabLit Quarterly*. Extracts from her diaries have been performed by Yusra Warsama at the Barbican Theatre, London, and Sama Rantisi at the Belgrade Theatre, Coventry. Her piece 'We Kill Terrorism' was read by Maxine Peake to a crowd of 15,000 protesters outside the 2024 Labour Party Conference in Liverpool.

To Omar, the kind soul, who held on to meaning
when words broke down under the weight of loss.

To those this wide world couldn't hold,
so heaven opened its arms for you.

To the ones who left, but whose voices still guide us,
laying down the ink of survival,
and building a shelter out of feeling.

These words are a testimony of resistance, and of the fact
that we are still here, writing, loving and pushing to live.

RAIN AND OLIVE TREES

IT'S RAINING, AND I love rainy mornings.

October rain is particularly eagerly anticipated by Palestinians, especially my father—he's on tenterhooks for it. People consider the rain a sign from Mother Nature, signalling the start of the *jad al-zaytoun* season, the olive harvest, in which the bond between the land and the people is renewed, and families gather to pick olives in an atmosphere of cooperation and joy.

My grandfather, Saleem Khalil Sabra, was born in 1897, before the establishment of Israel and before the British Mandate. He spent much of his life planting his land with olive and prickly pear trees. My family name 'Sabra' comes from the Arabic word for the prickly pear tree and our reputation for planting them. My grandfather established our orchards over 80 years ago, and when he passed away in 1994 (after living a long life, nearly 100 years) my father and his brothers pledged to care for the orchards as if the trees were their own children.

'The olive tree is like Palestine,' my grandfather used to say. 'Its roots burrow deep into the earth. Its branches are a symbol of peace. Its oil is the elixir of life.'

Despite all the colonisers' attempts to steal his land, the Palestinian clings to every last inch of it, facing the Israeli thirst for annihilation with an even more steadfast determination for life; dying a thousand times, if necessary, only to rise back up with a new-found love for the homeland.

Every October, our family, from the youngest to the eldest, prepares for the *jad al-zaytoun* season. I have a big family: twelve sisters and two brothers. This year, my father has bought a new ladder, and my eight-year-old brother Mahmoud has fetched a large, elegant glass bottle to fill with olive oil and give to his schoolfriend, Aisha. Yes, in Palestine, we give olive oil as a gift and a symbol: a present for a friend, a reward for success, a blessing for a bride.

As for myself, I try to convince my father to buy a new tea kettle, but he insists on keeping the old one — so charred by years of fire that it's now completely black. My father cherishes his things; he's the same with his relationships.

He always says, 'The dearest things I own in this life are my land, my library and you: my children.'

I'll let you in on a secret: throughout my childhood I felt jealous of my father's library.

I used to chide him, 'The dearest things you own in this life are me, me and me . . . *then* your books. I'll donate all your books to my school if you don't accept that.'

'I'll donate you,' he'd reply, jokingly. 'Or better still, I'll sell you and buy more books with the money.'

During the *jad al-zaytoun* season, the task of picking olives is as tiring as it is enjoyable. Tasks are divided among family members: one spreads mats on the ground, another picks olives from low-hanging branches, another climbs a ladder to reach the higher branches and yet another prepares breakfast — usually skiving the bulk of the work to sip a cup of tea and wait for the others to join them.

Others use machines or even chemicals to harvest their olives, but our family still picks by hand, a method insisted on by my late grandfather. My father says this method is gentlest on the tree and yields the richest oil. But the highest quality olives are those which fall on their own or with a gentle shake of the branches — these are sent to be pickled, rather than pressed.

Mats under the trees will catch everything that falls, including large, old and sick leaves. These leaves will be separated from the olives with a large sieve, or by the waft of a palm frond.

But all of this is to come.

Our visit today is largely to prepare for the season. We won't start picking today until everything is ready.

This morning, my four-year-old sister, Fatima, wakes up at 5:30am and doesn't allow anyone to go back to sleep. The whole family has to wake up once she's up, and no one dares to break this rule, not even Oscar the cat.

We prepare for the busy day ahead, loading the necessary items for the season into the car: ladder, ground mats, cooking pots. We haven't even had our morning coffee yet; we'll have it on the land when we arrive.

In the car, I receive a message from my writer friend Mahmoud El Basyouni, reminding me of our upcoming meeting. Mahmoud and I first met in 2020, at an event commemorating the anniversary of the passing of the poet Fadwa Tuqan.[1] Over time, our relationship developed, and in 2023 we launched a creative writing initiative for students of al-Daraj Neighbourhood Girls' School. Now, Mahmoud is publishing a sequel to his first novel, and we are planning to launch it at the YMCA on al-Jala'a Street.[2]

As soon as we reach our land, explosions echo in the distance, rattling off in time to our quickening heartbeats.

What is this? Is it a new war launched by Israel? Didn't they have enough bloodshed in previous wars and escalations?

But these rockets are coming from Gaza!

Is it a mistake in the resistance's missile system?

My questions are interrupted by the screams of my little sister Fatima. I hug her tightly and try to calm her down, but I can't seem to ease the shock.

I know this fear well. I lived with it throughout my own childhood. My lungs can't forget it, the smell of gunpowder[3] still lingers within them.

This is what it's like for Gazan children. Alongside the alphabet of letters, we learn the alphabet of wars. I was only eight years old when my own heart was tested on this subject. We were in the Arabic Language Test Hall when explosions began to thunder around us, creeping closer and closer to my school. The words 'war', 'escalation' and 'conflict' weren't yet in my vocabulary; I didn't understand the subtle differences between them as we poured out from our desks into the rows between exam tables, then into the corridors of the school, screaming and stumbling. Panic gripped everyone that day. I saw my teacher crying and trembling with fear. Then I knew it was serious.

That was in late December 2008, when Israel launched a bloodthirsty war on Gaza, killing over 200 Palestinians on the first day alone. In that war, Israel used white phosphorus for the first time, despite it being banned internationally.[4] They even used it in an attack on the UNRWA-run Fakhoura School, killing 40 civilians.[5] They have reused it in all subsequent wars on Gaza.

On the day of that attack, I wanted a hug from my mother. I remember needing it so badly. So today, in the orchard, I don't leave Fatima for a moment.

Quickly, we decide to pack up and return home, to leave the harvesting for another day, when things have calmed down. On the way back, passersby exchange a rumour about one of the prominent Hamas leaders being assassinated by Israel and Hamas launching rockets in response. This wouldn't surprise me. Israel has a long history of assassinating leaders, figureheads and even academics and poets like Ghassan Kanafani.[6] No Palestinian is safe. The very existence of any Palestinian — man, woman or child — is unsettling for Israel.

My brother suggests we go grocery shopping and buy a week's load of emergency supplies in case we're not able to leave the house for a few days. We do just this, grabbing everything we think we might need: meat, frozen food, cheese and a large quantity of vegetables, chickpeas and fava beans.

My friend Mahmoud and I postpone our meeting. Uncertainty prevails. For someone like me, who's mad about planning, this chaos is disturbing. Life is full of surprises at the best of times, but Gaza's surprises never end. And they're all unpleasant.

October 13, 2023

AN EMERGENCY BAG

This morning is unlike any other. The war rages without pause and the house is crowded. My eldest sister, Umm Arafah,[7] has arrived with her children and grandchildren; her own home has been badly damaged by the Israeli airstrikes.

We've woken early to prepare breakfast. I sit in front of the dough board, next to my little Fatoum (as I affectionately call Fatima). My task is to spread the cheese, thyme and oil onto the dough. Fatima watches and mimics my movements with childish curiosity.

Fatima and I share a birth month; we've always celebrated together with joy, cake and laughter. Fatima overflows with tender innocence and endearing mischief. There's a gleam in her light brown eyes. Her name, to me, is a warm melody — it echoes the name of my mother, who left this world too early.

When the dough is ready, my father takes over with skilled hands. The aroma of the pastries fills the air, and as the first batch emerges from the oven, I grab a few, pair them with a cup of sage tea, and retreat to my room to finish the film I started watching last night. I'm not sure if I'm escaping the noise of the kitchen, or arranging a truce with my own inner tension.

Perhaps this moment of solitude is a warrior's break: the temporary withdrawal of a weary fighter who needs to catch her breath without removing her armour.

As soon as I sit on my bed, Oscar the cat leaps up beside me, sensing I need his silent companionship. His presence is part of the ritual I'm clinging to.

One scene in the film shows a woman trying to get the hero's attention by walking back and forth in front of him while he sits engrossed in his newspaper, oblivious to her efforts. The scene stirs something in me, evoking a strange sorrow for women who expose their hearts to such neglect.

Immediately, I think of Yasmeen: my closest friend and the mirror through which I've often understood myself and the world. Yasmeen believes that love can't be seized or begged for; that it should flow like a clear river, without appointments or bargains. She rejects the idea of turning cartwheels for someone's attention. She says anyone who can't see you in your quietness doesn't deserve your noise.

I watch the scene again, still believing that femininity is best expressed in stillness, not in chasing; and that boldness, though beautiful, loses some of its balance when it comes from a woman.

My thoughts are interrupted by the arrival of my sister Asma's husband. He has returned from an emergency meeting with UNRWA. He tells us that Israel has declared Northern Gaza a military zone, that UNRWA staff are already being ordered to evacuate. It's deeply unsettling to think such a respected international agency is preparing to leave thousands of ordinary Palestinians behind; it hints at something far worse ahead.

At noon, the sky is filled with leaflets, falling like autumn leaves. We rush to the roof to watch them. They're warnings from the Israeli Army, instructing everyone in the North to evacuate immediately.

The leaflets read:

> *For your safety, take the upcoming opportunity to move*
> *south of Wadi Gaza. If you care about yourself and your*
> *loved ones, head south in accordance with our instructions.*

Israel is demanding that over a million residents of Gaza City evacuate and head south! How can they order us to leave our homes so easily? Where should we go? And how long will we remain displaced?

I climb down from the roof, and the moment I enter the house, massive explosions shake the walls and cause the ground beneath my feet to crack. Fear roots itself in our hearts. The screams of children and women grow louder. Fatima flings herself into my arms, clinging as if my embrace can shield her from the madness.

My father fears a repeat of the 1948 Nakba, when hundreds of thousands of Palestinians were forced to leave their land with no guarantee of return. These politicians seem to believe they have the right to determine our fate, to march us over the horizon of an unknown future and reduce our choice to dying in our homes or leaving everything behind.

What absurdity.

My father suggests the children and most of the women should follow the occupation's orders and evacuate to the South. He and a few men will stay behind temporarily, he says, to guard our possessions.

The prospect of separation in such tense circumstances frightens me. I try to convince my father to let me stay, but he refuses. I've never seen him so stern, so angry, so afraid.

Back in my room, I grab my phone to tell Yasmeen I'll be leaving soon.

For a moment, she meets me with silence, as if searching for the right words. Then her voice comes through, soft and full of worry, as though words alone won't carry the weight of her emotion.

'Are you sure?' she asks.

Yasmeen's family are leaning towards staying; they have no relatives in the South, no places to stay. I think Yasmeen is trying to stop me leaving, too, but all she can do is repeat in a trembling voice: 'I can't bear the thought of you being far away.'

'The circumstances are beyond our control,' I reply, trying to reassure her with a calm tone, while feeling nothing but uncertainty. 'I'll stay in touch, always.'

I don't believe what I'm saying.

Displacement is a leap into the unknown. You abandon everything you love and cram your life into an emergency bag. As I prepare mine, I wonder: what can it possibly hold? How can a bag contain everything that makes this place home?

My wardrobe holds several formal outfits, purchased for my planned master's degree in International Relations. For a moment, I think about taking them. I love them, just as I love the trophies I've collected from school poetry and writing competitions. But neither belong in this new reality.

Instead, I pack my personal documents and educational certificates, holding on to a few small items that might remind me of the life I'm leaving: my pens, my colouring pencils, this diary.

My father arranges for a minibus to take us south. We strap mattresses, blankets, bags and food to its roof — overloading it so heavily that I fear it might tip over. I ride with my sister Umm Arafah and her family, heading to a plot of farmland in Rafah, whose owner has kindly granted us permission to pitch tents. Fatima sits beside me, clutching her doll and calling it Joud: a name which reflects generosity and kindness.

Just as we begin to move, Fatima remembers the morning's pastries. We call for the driver to stop, and I collect the remaining pastries for her. She is thrilled.

The minibus takes us south on Salah al-Din Road: Gaza's main highway, stretching 25 miles from the Erez Crossing in the North to the Rafah Crossing in the South. Our driver follows the Israeli-designated 'safe corridor'. The road is extremely crowded and the minibus can only creep forwards in fits and starts, moving a few metres at a time before grinding to a halt again.

People are pouring out of Gaza City in their thousands: some in vehicles, others on foot. Many carry mattresses on their backs. Some herd livestock. Journalists and photographers are everywhere, documenting the moment.

Near Wadi Gaza [a dry riverbed which bisects the Gaza Strip], we pass a destroyed car, its parts scattered along the roadside. Emergency workers are gathering the dismembered remains of Palestinian civilians from inside and outside the vehicle. None of the bodies are intact. I cover Fatoum's eyes with my arm, shielding her from the horror.[8]

Just before sunset, we reach our destination: a piece of land in al-Miraj area: a quiet agricultural region, whose simple residents greet us with generosity, cold water and warm bread.

This piece of land is vast, mostly dry and dotted with shrubs. A lone fig tree casts a long and gentle shadow. The odour of a cattle farm wafts through the air. In a corner of the land stands a small, makeshift bathroom, its door: a battered zinc sheet. Its wooden floor barely fit to stand on.

The sting of cold here reminds me of the breeze which often blew across my bedroom balcony at home. But in Rafah, the breeze isn't welcome. Not when we're forced to sleep in a tent.

Not when we're exposed to the elements. Tonight, the breeze, like so many things, is another of Gaza's unpleasant surprises.

This day will be forever etched in my memory, like the first day of a new job, or a first love, or the first taste of bitter loss. But displacement is unique in its abruptness. There's no rehearsal, no preparation. You must let go of almost everything you cherish and set out on a path that's jagged and desolate, as if you had never been tied to anything at all.

October 25, 2023

TO GAZA

A few days after we arrived in Rafah, we were joined by my father and the men of my family. Our reunion was warm, and filled with mixed emotions. The security we'd lost was temporarily restored. The presence of men provided more than emotional support, it has become a necessity in these unstable and exceptional circumstances, especially when we, the women, find ourselves living in an area without easy access to markets or essential services.

After the men arrived, each household of our family decided to pitch their tent in a different corner of the land, hoping to maintain some privacy and order. Despite the simplicity of our surroundings, we endeavoured to create some semblance of life, however fragile it might be.

I start my day with heaps of laundry, washing them by hand in two large containers. My little duck Fatoum plays and splashes next to me, laughing each time the water touches her face, or her hand brushes a piece of colourful cloth.

I scrub everything carefully, feeling for cleanliness, then I move each item to the second container to rinse in clean water. Piece by piece, container by container, the huge pile begins to diminish.

At noon, my sister Raghda calls us from Gaza City. She's spoken to her doctor, who's confirmed she is pregnant. This news is a surprise and a joy, but it also brings anxiety. Her pregnancy isn't stable, and she needs someone to stay by her side, someone to take care of her. So she asks my father to send me back to Gaza City.

When the car arrives to collect me, I embrace my father tightly.

'Be well, my love,' I say.

I take my little brother Mahmoud in my arms and kiss him. 'Take care of yourself and Baba. You're a hero.'

My father pulls a wad of money from his pocket and offers it to me.

I hold up my hand. 'No need, I have enough.'

'Take it,' he replies, 'and don't argue with me.'

I kiss his head and leave.

I've sent Fatoum on an errand, so she doesn't have to see me leave. Saying goodbye wouldn't be easy for her.

As we drive north again on Salah al-Din Road, I feel a deep sadness, as though my heart is still anchored to my father. But there's also some joy: my return to Gaza City, despite all its destruction and danger, is a small victory over fear, displacement and the idea that we might be forced to leave our homes forever.

When I arrive, I go straight to our house in the Sabra neighbourhood and call my friend Yasmeen. She excitedly replies that she'll come over immediately.

I enter my room. Everything is as I left it: every detail, every scent. I take Oscar the cat from his little bag, and as soon as his feet touch the floor, he begins to prance around the room, sniffing everything, reassuring himself of his own memories. He stops beside his little cat house, and approaches it slowly, as if he, too, has returned from a long exile.

41

I stand in front of the mirror, seeing my face clearly for the first time in days. I stare for a long time, then I wash my face with cold water, pluck my excess hair and take a warm shower.

Despite the destruction visible everywhere, my return feels like a long embrace. The city may not be safe, but it is home.

The doorbell rings. It's Yasmeen.

I open the door, and shout with excitement, 'Ta-dah, I'm back!'

'Scaredy cat! Running away? Afraid of dying, huh?'

We hug tightly.

Yasmeen says, 'I've missed you. These days without you haven't been nice!'

'Honestly, I didn't miss you much. The sun of Rafah dried up my feelings and dried my skin too!' Then I laugh and add, 'I missed you so much, my friend!'

A little while later, the doorbell rings again. I'm not expecting anyone. To our surprise we find my sister Randa, holding a plate of maftoul [couscous].

'Welcome,' I say, 'and welcome to what you're carrying!'

Randa, my caring sister, is a skilful chef with unbeatable recipes. We all sit together, eating, and drinking sage tea.

With my visitors gone, I grab my bag and head to Raghda's house, where I plan to live during her pregnancy. Raghda is like another parent to me: so kind in a way that reminds me of our mother. The moment she sees me, she hugs me — our embrace is full of prayer, tears and thanks for our safety.

At this moment, news begins to circulate about a possible ground invasion on Salah al-Din Road. My sense of gratitude deepens: I've arrived just ahead of the danger, as though something or someone had been watching over me on my journey. I believe it was my father's prayers.

November 24, 2023

REST FROM THE SHADOW OF DEATH

At 7am today, a truce came into effect after 49 days of bombardment. It is not a metaphor but a fact to say that Israel tried to wring death out of every last second. The news of the martyrdom of Mohammed Al-Bayadh and Noaman Al-Bayadh, prominent sons of al-Daraj neighbourhood, came just ten minutes before the truce began. Mohammed had gone for the Fajr prayer at the Saad Ibn Mo'ath Mosque when the Israeli planes bombed it, bringing the building down on the heads of the worshippers. When his brother Noaman heard the news, he rushed to the Mosque to try to save Mohammed, but the Israeli planes returned and bombed the area again.

The Saad Ibn Mo'ath Mosque was not just a place for prayer. It also housed a huge generator which supplied the neighbourhood with electricity for one hour each day, and effectively supplied the neighbourhood with water too (as the water tanks relied on electric pumps for refilling).

I stood on the roof of my sister's house in al-Sahaba Street, watching a huge crowd of people trying to lift the rubble with their hands, searching for their loved ones. With each person they pulled out, someone would cry 'Martyr! Martyr!' and the crowd would loudly chant 'Allahu Akbar! Allahu Akbar!'

Mohammed and Noaman's uncle arrived at the site and sat weeping under a tree. Another man came and told him that his nephews were gone. As I watched, the number of martyrs increased to twelve. Everyone pulled from under the rubble was dead. But there were still people missing: either dead or wounded.

After a few minutes, I came down from the roof to tell Raghda what I'd seen.

'I knew Mohammed,' my sister replied. 'He was a kind boy; he helped me carry water upstairs many times.'

'May God have mercy on him,' I said, and after a few moments of silence in the presence of death, I added: 'I'll prepare to return to our family home in al-Sabra. I miss it. I miss the rose plants on the balconies. Have they withered? I miss my room, especially my bed.'

'Let's wait,' Raghda said. 'Israel might break the truce, and we could get hurt.'

'So be it,' I replied. 'I don't care!'

As we left my sister's house, we saw the bodies of Mohammed and Noaman surrounded by a crowd of people performing the burial rites. Their mother sat at the head of Noaman, her youngest son, clutching his shroud, and saying, 'Wasn't one enough? Both of them! Why am I not with you?'

Her husband held her and tried to wipe away her tears. They both broke down crying together.

Mohammed, their eldest, had been tall and broad. But in his shroud, Mohammed was the size of a one-year-old child. His body had melted, and they had only found his head, parts of his limbs and a few kilograms of his flesh. But at least, as one neighbour put it, he was lucky to have received the prayers of the men from the neighbourhood; lucky he would be buried in a grave, not abandoned for stray dogs to feast on.

Have you ever heard of people comparing the luck of one death to another?

Recently, my eight-year-old niece Abeer said to me, 'I hope I die instantly so I don't feel anything, and that no part of me gets amputated. I always pray not to get maimed. I want a quick death, all at once. And you, Auntie, how do you want to die?'

As we reach al-Sabra neighbourhood, the streets are filled with people, most walking on foot, carrying their bedding and belongings. Whenever someone meets someone they know, they shake hands as if it's a holiday, thanking God for the safety of their neighbours and relatives.

'Are you still alive?' I hear one passerby say to another. 'The good people die, and those like you live!'

It is a heavy joke, but the recipient laughs loudly.

The joy of survival stirs something in me. If Fatoum were here, I would run to her, lift her in my arms, throw her into the air and catch her again, kissing her a thousand times.

The city no longer looks familiar. Destruction has altered its appearance, like a scene from a horror movie. Most of the buildings are damaged. The cars seem to have emerged from a fierce battle. Most people have replaced them with animal-drawn carts.

The streets resemble a poor, dishevelled man from another era, clad in tattered clothes and stared at with disdain. Navigating them requires physical fitness: you must scale mountains of rubble from destroyed buildings, then descend through deep valleys quarried by crazed rockets determined to abolish life and infrastructure. Electric pylons lie on the ground. Manhole covers gape open. With my own eyes, I see the remnants of missiles and bombs marked 'Made in America' and 'Made in India'. Has the entire world united to kill us?

When our family home comes into view, my anxiety slowly eases. My father spent a lifetime building this home; I've been so afraid we'd lose it. I love my own room in particular; the best thing about it is that it's mine; I have the freedom to choose its decor, paint and furniture. It also overlooks a delightful balcony, on which I've often planted roses, geraniums and seedlings such as basil and mint.

Now, the doors to my room and my father's room are broken, along with all the windows. Some of the walls have been damaged by small pieces of shrapnel. I hate how the occupation treats our homes: as if they're just buildings made of stone, when they're so much more than that. But, despite everything, I'm glad the damage isn't worse. In this long-awaited moment

I can lie on my bed and sleep like a mischievous child, worn out from a long day of playing.

If time could stop here, I wouldn't mind.

December 7, 2023

'WE KILL TERRORISM'

Of course, they don't *intend* to kill us, even when they drop 2,000-pound bombs on us. Even when they rain down bombardments across entire neighbourhoods and make life impossible in our city. No, no, don't misunderstand. They are merely eradicating 'terrorism.'

Two days ago, on December 5, 'terrorism' was hiding in the body of Omar, my six-year-old nephew, perhaps in his heart, or maybe among his soft locks of hair. So they killed him. They dropped two missiles on him and his siblings, Aya and Ahmad and his niece Sila, who was only seven months old, killing them all.

At 5am, my sister Randa woke to strange noises outside her house in Shuja'iyya. She roused her husband Saeed to investigate, and as soon as he opened the window, two successive explosions shook him. A thick layer of smoke filled the air outside.

Fearing a sniper might be hiding in the surrounding buildings, my sister Randa fell to the floor, and crawled towards the adjacent room, in which her children had been sleeping. She found them all awake, and whispered in the ear of her eldest son, Samir, 'The army has surrounded us.'

Fear gripped Samir's heart; he picked up his own seven-month-old daughter, Sila, kissed her and put his hand over her mouth to prevent any sound that might alert the Israeli soldiers. Saeed suggested they go down to the basement and wait for the Israelis to withdraw from the area. But as soon as they descended the stairs, shells hit the courtyard of the house, forcing them to flee.

The sun was already rising as they moved cautiously towards the backyard, which led out into the street. There were eleven people in total: Randa and her husband Saeed; their children Samir, Mohammed, Ahmad, Aya, Fella, Farah and Omar; as well as Samir's wife Saja and their baby daughter Sila. They snuck into the garden one by one, holding white flags over their heads. The air smelt of gunpowder. A dense fog enveloped the neighbourhood. Sounds of cannons echoed on all sides. They picked up speed and headed for a side street, about ten metres wide.

A quadcopter drone,[9] flying low over the rooftops, noticed them and rained its bullets down on them. They scattered, stumbled, fell to the ground thinking it was all over, then realising they were still alive, got back to their feet and fled with all their might, driven by the profoundest of instincts: survival. Randa, Saeed,and one of their daughters, Fella, ran into a house at the end of the street, seeking refuge.

The others kept running, cleaving to the walls for cover. Nowhere was safe in the neighbourhood. Eventually they reached an UNRWA school, but the missiles had followed them. How must it have felt to have reached the verge of safety — to be able to smell survival — only to have death pounce again as they rounded the corner?

My six-year-old nephew Omar was struck in the head by a piece of shrapnel and died instantly. His brother Ahmad, sister Aya and baby niece Sila were wounded and bleeding. This was Omar's first year in elementary school. He never got to memorise the route to school each morning, or to mischievously ring doorbells and run away before anyone came. He chose another path, a more peaceful one: to soar with the flocks of young pigeons to the skies above Gaza.

With the help of a neighbour, Samir dragged his siblings to a nearby house, where he tried every possible way to stop their bleeding. Aya was wounded in her side; Ahmad in his chest and legs. Samir ran back into the street, trying to find an ambulance, though he himself had sustained a shrapnel injury to his throat and lost a tooth in his lower jaw. His efforts proved futile. Thousands of wounded are left to die on the pavements or in their houses because there just aren't enough ambulances.

When I received the news, I tried to contact the Red Cross, struggling with the signal before finally getting through.

'Hello habibti, Red Cross here, how can we help you?'

'This is Sondos, I need an ambulance to transport my sister's children to the hospital. They are trapped in Shuja'iyya in a house belonging to...'

'We are sorry, habibti, we cannot help. The Israeli Army is preventing our personnel from entering Shuja'iyya.'

How cold the answer.

How warm the blood.

After an hour of bleeding, Ahmad followed his brother Omar. Minutes later, Aya joined them.

The neighbour wrapped their bodies in bedcovers and placed them on the second floor of the house, away from the eyes of his own children. At the same time, Samir's daughter Sila was clinging to life as long as possible, craving more of her mother's hugs, craving more of her father's kisses.

Sila was the first grandchild of my sister Randa's family. Her arrival brought joy to the entire household. Everyone had participated in setting up her room, equipping it with everything a baby might need. The day of her birth had been a celebration; her father distributed sweets to all the children and adults of the neighbourhood, rejoicing.

During the November truce, I visited Sila, took her in my arms and breathed in her scent. That day, a tiny white tooth started to press upwards in her lower gums. True, it hadn't fully protruded, but it already felt sharp, voraciously biting any finger that dared touch it. Sila had a laugh that would melt your soul, transporting you out of your own dull world and into hers, with all its exuberance.

After twelve hours of bleeding, she decided to let go of this world: a world that had turned its back on her.

Until we meet again, summer fruit.

Sila's body remained in the arms of her mother, Saja, for a whole day. Due to the ongoing fighting in the neighbourhood, Saja and Samir were unable to leave the house to bury Sila, Aya, Ahmad or Omar.

Saja was injured too: one piece of shrapnel had embedded itself in her right elbow, another in her left leg. She was barely able to move. The neighbour's wife tried everything she could to persuade Saja to let go of her daughter, so she could place Sila's body with the bodies of the other children on the upper floor.

Saja refused. 'Please, let her stay in my arms; I want to hold her for longer.'

Saja married at eighteen, gave birth at nineteen and has lost her daughter before turning twenty. How can her young heart bear this amount of anguish? And to have this compounded by the pain of milk drying in her breasts.

While this tragedy unfolded, my sister Randa, her husband Saeed and their daughter Fella were still trapped in the house they had sought refuge in, unable to leave, and unaware of their children's martyrdom. They'd tried calling Samir and Saja several times in the night, but their network was down. It's common for the Israelis to cut off communications in the areas they've invaded.

Randa, Saeed and Fella were not alone in the house they'd taken refuge in. Over 40 people were trapped with them, all without food and water. After a full day under siege, the tanks were getting closer, and the thick smell of gunpowder made breathing almost impossible. A shell hit the roof of the house, causing a fire to break out on the upper floors. Those trapped inside could no longer bear waiting for death, so they decided to flee, though danger surrounded them. They left with white flags raised, but the Israeli soldiers fired at them regardless. Some fell as martyrs, while others were injured. It was only through God's will that Randa, Saeed and Fella survived, fleeing through empty streets and desperately searching for their family.

Eventually, Saeed spotted one of his neighbours, Abu Sami, peeking cautiously through a window in his door.

'Thank God you're safe,' Saeed said. 'Have you seen my children? Are they with a neighbour?'

'I've heard Abu Ahmad's house holds the injured and displaced, they might have information about your children,' Abu Sami replied. 'But I wouldn't advise you to wander around the neighbourhood. Most of the houses are abandoned, and there are drones shooting at anyone who moves.'

Saeed, Randa and Fella ran towards Abu Ahmad's house, their hearts pounding violently in their chests. As soon as they arrived, Saeed shouted, 'Are my children with you Abu Ahmad?'

Abu Ahmad did not respond.

Saeed asked again, 'Where are my children?'

In a hoarse voice, Abu Ahmad answered, 'Say: there is no god but God.'

With force, my sister Randa pushed the door open, and entered to find her daughter-in-law, Saja, holding Sila's body and weeping bitterly.

'Sila's dead!' Saja screamed. 'They're all gone, no one is left!'

Randa froze. She didn't scream or cry; she just stared at Sila, stared for a long time.

Fella dropped to her knees. 'It's impossible! She's just asleep! Sila, my heart, wake up! I'll bring you a strawberry lollipop!'

Another neighbour approached and hugged Randa, saying through her tears, 'May God give you patience...May God take revenge.'

Through broken breaths, Randa asked, 'Where are my children?'

The neighbour pointed: 'Upstairs.'

When he reached the upper floor, Saeed staggered as if he had lost his senses. He kneeled and lifted the covers from the faces of his children one by one, pulling each child to his chest. He let out a suppressed wail, painful and deep, as if his heart had silently exploded—a muted groan emerging from a wound so deep the entire world couldn't heal it.

Randa stood by Omar, her beloved boy, wiping his small, cold face. Still, she did not cry or scream. She only whispered, in a broken voice, 'My darling...You can not know how much I love you. Why did they do this to you?'

Beside Omar lay Ahmad, a quiet and shy child who had lost the hearing in his left ear at the age of five. He didn't like running and playing like other children his age; he preferred watching anime and imitating his favourite characters with great skill. Randa kissed his little hands and placed them on her face. 'Oh, my soul, my child, you are leaving me too. Forgive me, my darling, I couldn't protect you!'

And Aya, their sister...When I first heard about Aya's injury, I deeply hoped it was minor. I considered Aya a friend as much as I considered her my niece. She was athletic, strong, full of life. Naively, I believed that someone like her couldn't die. Life suited her so well; she knew how to live it.

Death is a reality, I don't deny it. But I never imagined I would lose Aya in such a brutal way.

Fella and Aya were more than just sisters. Fella, the youngest of the pair, saw Aya as her guide in the difficult aspects of life: the friend who would always be by her side. Sometimes, I felt annoyed by Fella's tendency to copy everything Aya did. Sometimes, I would tell her, 'You need to be yourself, not Aya's shadow.'

But over time, I saw what Aya meant to Fella. She was more than a sister; she was her life itself, her source of strength, her place of refuge.

Fella placed her head next to Aya's, holding her sister's body with boundless tenderness. She stayed by her side all night, lost in deep silence, unable to believe she was losing this part of herself forever.

By sunrise, Fella's clothes were soaked in Aya's blood, even her hair was laced with it, but she felt nothing except emptiness. Everything around her was silent. The sounds of the artillery and drones no longer mattered.

This morning, news arrived that the occupation's vehicles had pulled back slightly. The neighbours took this opportunity to move the injured and recover the bodies of the martyrs. No medical help was available. In a desperate effort, the locals tried to move the injured in horse-drawn carts, hoping to reach al-Ahli Baptist Hospital: a temporary refuge for the wounded since the larger al-Shifa Hospital was attacked.

As for my sister's children: they were buried in a hurry, with no chance to say goodbye. No funeral honoured their dignity; no shrouds preserved their bodies. They were buried in the covers they had lain in, to sleep in the peace they were deprived of in reality. Our consolation is that they are now in the gardens of Paradise.

Who knows, perhaps terrorism hides in the warmth of a home, in the bells of churches or the minarets of mosques, between the pages of books, in the streets and alleyways of the camps, or even amidst the tents of the displaced. The Israeli occupation has every right to erase anything from the face of the Earth, if they so desire. And no one has the right to criticise Israel.

After all, they are saving humanity from the evildoers.

How valiant of them.

How noble.

January 6, 2024

SLEEP DURING WARTIME IS ELUSIVE

Sleep during wartime is elusive, the search for it is like the search for a loaf of bread. Low-flying planes emit a never-ending buzz, and I wonder: does their fuel ever run out? Do their pilots tire of bombing and surveilling? Are they ever tempted to grant just one Gazan a night of peaceful sleep?

Gunfire and explosions echo sporadically. Any one of those bullets is capable of rending my body to shreds. Any one of those missiles is capable of levelling an entire neighbourhood. In my head there's another sound, no less tumultuous than the buzz of war, and audible above the gunfire and confusion — the buzz of questions such as:

Will tragedy befall my family in Rafah?

Will I see my little sister Fatima again?

Is our separation permanent?

Am I the next target?

Our home has become overcrowded, sheltering family and displaced people alike. Among those here now are Randa and Saeed, with their surviving children; Raghda, with her daughter and in-laws; two of my cousins and their wives; and the family of my friend Yasmeen. The men sleep in the living room, the women in the central corridor — all of us stretched out on mattresses in neat rows, like bodies in a mass grave, enveloped in darkness.

On my first night in the corridor, the 30 or so people taking refuge in our home crowded my thoughts. I wondered how so many of us could share the guest bathroom. (The main bathroom was rendered unusable when shrapnel pierced the sewage pipes, causing wastewater to leak into the street and neighbouring houses.) After lying awake for some time, I got up from my mattress, using the light of my phone to guide me, but was stopped by an older woman known as Umm Khaled.

'Put down the phone, child, you'll get us all killed!' she scolded. 'Don't you know there are snipers on the rooftops all around us?'

I returned to my place, a lump forming in my throat. I wanted to scream, as much at the old woman as at the snipers on the rooftops and the rest of the world.

Umm Khaled knew my grandfather, Saleem, and often speaks about him: telling me how he would visit her grandfather early in the morning, riding a white donkey and bringing a huge basket of figs. She has never tasted better figs, she says. I'm not exactly sure how Umm Khaled feels about me now. Often, I feel she loves me; or rather, she loves my family. At other times she can't stand the sight of me because I don't follow her instructions.

In the mornings, Umm Khaled recounts stories of battles past and present, detailing the many different risks resistance fighters take every day, as if she were one herself. She obsesses over the devil that she calls the mobile phone, how it exposes civilians and fighters alike, making them vulnerable with its bright screen and traceable signals. She forbids its use.

Most likely, the old lady is channelling some of the psychological trauma of war through a distrust of technology and an abiding belief that all corruption stems from this single advancement: the phone. But for me, my phone is a lifeline. Whenever I feel lonely, I open its gallery and look at photos of Fatima, and

54

even though communications are down most of the time, there's always the hope that a message from my father will reach me, reassuring me that he and other members of my family are safe.

Warplanes launch their missiles day and night. Explosions in the early hours cast a pall of choking gases across our neighbourhood, their foul odour scraping at our throats, sometimes even claiming lives. No one knows what's in these gases. Their smell, reminiscent of sewage, seems to change every time. To think, I have made peace with these foul fumes. I no longer even cover my mouth and nose when I smell them.

At this time of year, the cold of night is biting. My hands and nose freeze. I wish we could light a fire to warm a little water, but my sisters have warned against it repeatedly. We know the enemy is indiscriminate; any fire or light could be a target for their warplanes.

I hear the sounds of clashes nearby. Time passes slowly, as if stretching in on itself so thinly it will disappear in the chaos of war. Each night, we wait for the morning as if it's a promise that might never be fulfilled. Each morning, we remain indoors until the day is fully bright, hoping the sun will provide some safety. As always, we keep a close eye on the news, listen out for gunshots and explosions and search for any glimmer of good news — from tracking the footsteps in the street below, to eavesdropping on others' conversations and opinions. Our thoughts swing pendulum-like between hope and anxiety.

Today, it seems a breakthrough is imminent. They say the enemy is withdrawing from the area. People go out to verify the news. A light scattering of movement spreads across the neighbourhood. Reassurance seeps back into our hearts, as if life is slowly returning.

The fear may have receded, but the queues at the bathroom door don't get any shorter. When it comes to my turn, I discover that the water ran out with the person in the eighth spot. I curse my luck and join a new queue, searching for a litre of water, to no avail. I feel the great sadness of our collective existence. If I were a cat, I wouldn't have to queue for water or wait for the world's sympathy to turn towards us. If I were a cat, I could eat from the earth's scraps and drink from its puddles.

The doorbell rings and I answer. Our neighbour stands in front of me, a ball of dough in his hands. He asks if he can use our wood-fired oven. I hesitate for a moment, then find myself agreeing in exchange for four litres of water. I'm ecstatic at the thought of being able to wash, but just as quickly saddened that we're bartering over such measly things. At one time, we boasted to the world of our generosity and chivalry.

At last, I start to wash my face, though I'm unable to avoid showing it to the mirror. Just then, I hear something crash to the ground in the kitchen as our neighbour flees. Before we know it, a missile screeches overhead. The walls shake, but the missile doesn't explode yet. Maybe it's a warning strike: identifying a location for a larger subsequent strike. Either way, its message couldn't be clearer: the withdrawal of tanks doesn't mean an end to the destruction.

Our neighbour's radio blares loudly, broadcasting the news that international pressure is being exerted on Israel to allow aid to enter, particularly from the United States.

'Our generous friends!' our neighbour comments sarcastically. 'They'll send aid while the waterfall of blood is still flowing!'

This friendly character once fashioned a spent bomb casing into his favourite ashtray, hollowing it out and inscribing it with the words 'Made in America'.

Now, he calls out to his wife, Saad, 'Add some sugar for goodness' sake. We've been married for twenty years, and you still haven't learnt how much sugar I like!'

'A kilo of sugar costs ten times its normal price, my dear,' Saad retorts. 'Your teacups alone need a pound of sugar a day. You have to get used to tea without it!'

They say humans can adapt and become accustomed to anything in this life. Perhaps Saad's husband will get used to tea without sugar, but how will Palestinians get used to what's really happened over the last few months: our city in ruins, our people stripped of their dignity? In the clearest possible language, this war has exhausted us, drained us, worn us down. We are nothing but oppressed in our own land, counting the days and misnaming them.

January 9, 2024

Oscar the cat spent last night in my arms, his breathing becoming more and more rapid. This morning, he passed away. There are no veterinary clinics available. Even leaving the house is difficult.

January 10, 2024

I am the only one who dares to sleep in my old bedroom: the room with the balcony. Some have called me reckless, others: crazy. Only Yasmeen, my friend, has called me courageous. But none of these labels is quite true. I'm not reckless, not courageous. I'm afraid, afraid to the bone.

The truth is that sleeping among so many bodies in the corridor is impossible. The heavy scent of sweat, overflowing baby's nappies, stifled whispers, rapid breaths: all of it is suffocating. I simply prefer the idea of dying while I'm still clean and pure.

Tonight, I'm dragging my mattress out of the corridor when one of the women interrupts me, her tone disapproving: 'Sleeping here would be safer for you!'

Umm Khaled responds, 'Leave her be, poor thing, she's just naive . . . Of course, if she had a grain of sense, she'd stay away from danger instead of playing with it!'

I ignore them both, and continue to my room where, under threat of snipers, I crawl towards the balcony, stretch an old Egyptian towel across the window and secure it with clothes pegs. Then, I tie some clothes together and hang them in front of the second window, not enough to block the view completely, but enough to prevent any light escaping. Finally, I pull my phone from under my blanket, despite the collective agreement to keep our phones off, and check the time. It feels as though the night is nearly over, but it's only 11:15pm.

A familiar whisper snaps me out of my thoughts. Yasmeen has slipped into the room, laughing softly.

'Did you really think I wouldn't follow you?' she asks. 'I'm with you till the end of time!'

The clothes in the window sway in the breeze. Israeli flares paint the darkness of the sky with flickering light.

'Oh wow, you're practically sitting at the border! Full HD view,' Yasmeen says.

I laugh. 'Better than the smell of sweat, girl. And if you ask me, being neighbours with Israel is better than being neighbours with Umm Khaled! My God, how annoying she is!'

We fall into a fit of laughter that leaves us almost breathless. Yasmeen alone has the ability to make the night less terrifying. She's been my friend since we were ten years old, and has been there for me during my life's most challenging moments, including the illness of my mother, may she rest in peace.

I sing to Yasmeen, as I always do when silence stretches between us, reciting the words of Tamim al-Barghouti:[10]

> *Oh Yasmeen who comes from Aleppo*
> *Your family is Turkish and mine are Arabs*

For your eyes I forgave the time
That I was blaming for so long

'Oh Yasmeen, I swear...'

'Sondos, you're making my search for a husband even harder. I need someone fluent in poetry and obsessed with language!'

'Do you want him to be handsome?'

'Of course!'

'And a chef who can cook?'

'Yes, and an entrepreneur too.'

'And an astronaut?'

'Obviously!'

'Then go to sleep,' I say. 'You'll find him in your dreams.'

January 11, 2024

This morning, we are woken at dawn by a knock on the door.

'Get up, girls! Make wudu and pray Fajr!'

A more insistent voice follows: 'Come on, wake up! Cast out the devil and put your trust in God!'

We are the last to wake up, which means we won't have to fight for space in the tiny bathroom.

After Fajr prayer, we begin our day as we have come to know it, though nothing in war ever truly feels normal. The women gather the mattresses and fold the blankets — some hastily, others sluggishly, as if delaying the start of yet another day. In the corner, Umm Khaled sits by the clay oven, skilfully baking shrak [unleavened flatbread], flipping the dough swiftly, lifting it with care and setting it aside to cool.

In the kitchen, a few women are gathering what little food they have managed to collect: a can of tuna from here, some fava beans from there, scraps of old cheese and Umm Khaled's bread. No one asks where the food has come from, or whether it will be enough. We know the answer already: it will last for today, and tomorrow if we're lucky. Breakfast is shared, just as everything has become shared: hunger, fear, even dreams.

At exactly 7am, the walls tremble with the blast of shelling and gunfire rains down from the balconies that surround us. In shock, we turn to the windows, as if waiting for the next strike, or perhaps for the end itself; then we hasten to gather in the narrow hallway, no more than fifteen metres in length, our bodies pressed against each other, seeking protection from the invisible threat lurking outside. Women's voices rise, blending with the cries of children.

My cousin enters, his voice steady. 'Say: there is no god but God.'

Everyone repeats: 'There is no god but God.'

'People, seek guidance from God. Nothing will happen to us except what He has decreed.'

'We put our trust in God.'

Jamil, my eight-year-old nephew, holds onto his mother with one hand while gripping his ten-year-old sister, Abeer, with the other. He says: 'Abeer, I'm sorry for throwing mud at you on our way home from school. Forgive me and ask God to forgive us.'

Abeer, expressionless, replies: 'I forgive you.'

'And Mama, when I threw mud at Abeer, you yelled at her because her clothes got dirty. You should apologise to her too.'

'I'm sorry, Abeer.'

They obey Jamil as though he is their teacher, fear silencing their usual defiance.

Outside, the shelling intensifies, until a violent knock shakes our front door. We open it to a masked man with a green band tied around his head [the attire of a Hamas fighter].

'You need to evacuate immediately,' the man says. 'The occupation's tanks are advancing towards your homes. Leave now!'

Everyone is frozen in shock. The man begins picking up children and carrying them in his arms, soothing them as he guides us outside. We follow him. His comrades are knocking on neighbours' doors, urging them to flee, handing out dates and water, directing people to safer routes.

Then, suddenly, they vanish.

We start to run. The air is thick with gunpowder. I help the mothers carry their children, feeling, for a moment, lucky to be free from the weight of parental responsibility. Yet, at the same time, I feel a deep duty towards my sister's children, as if they have been entrusted to me.

Chaos and terror reign. Conversations are frantic, breaths laboured, faces covered in layers of dust. We are fleeing with nothing but the clothes on our backs. I didn't even close the door to our home.

Death is so close. At one point, I had wished for it. But now, as I run, my desire to survive is genuine.

January 12, 2024

A THRESHOLD OF SAFETY

Yesterday, after running for miles, we arrived at a school: Ahmad Shawqi Secondary School, the very school I graduated from in 2017, now a shelter for displaced people.

I don't know why, but a shiver of dread ran through me as we entered the compound, even though the chaos flooding the place had nothing to do with the disciplined atmosphere I remember from my school days.

I could hear the voice of my old headmistress ringing in my ears: 'Girls! No makeup! Stick to the uniform! Keep your nails trimmed at all times!'

If one of us so much as dared to wear a bit of eyeliner or mascara, the headmistress would unleash a torrent of scolding: 'Foolish girls! You think there's a groom waiting for you at the school gates?'

Ironically, the headmistress plastered her own face in cosmetics and almost always wore high heels, which clicked noisily as she stalked the school corridors, searching for prey.

As a student, I was often lined up among the latecomers, not out of carelessness, but because my mother had been diagnosed with kidney failure and could no longer move. After my sister Shireen's marriage, the responsibility of caring for my mother fell entirely on my shoulders, almost overnight. My mother's dialysis sessions began at six in the morning. After making sure one of my older sisters had arrived to relieve me, I would rush off to school.

Upon arrival, I was often greeted by the headmistress herself. 'Ah, Sabra, you're late again today!'

I never had the heart to explain. Shame tied my tongue.

The headmistress would scan me from head to toe with a sharp gaze and mutter: 'Go on to your class...and don't be late again.'

Now, the school is crammed with displaced families. In the hallways, they've strung up clotheslines. In every corner of the staircases, they're burning small fires, blackening the walls with soot. No doors or windows remain intact; all have been shattered by the bombings, replaced by fluttering pieces of cloth. One toilet serves dozens of families. Piles of rubbish clog the schoolyard.

When we arrived, no classrooms were left for us to claim as a home. Each room was filled with displaced people. All of them were taken, except for the science lab. My brother-in-law Nael pushed at the lab door, once, twice...till it finally gave way, revealing a mountain of scattered furniture, broken desks, smashed windows and laboratory equipment strewn everywhere.

Reality pressed down on me like a boulder, as though everything around me was determined to break my spirit. This place, once a theatre for education and discipline, had become a haven for chaos and sorrow.

Perhaps my need for privacy and solitude, amidst a sea of death and destruction, sounds like a foolish indulgence against the logic of survival. But inwardly, my spirit was choking, my mind screaming: *I can't take it! I can't endure being a homeless wretch, stripped of all life.*

I called my father, utterly broken.

I have always tried to be strong in front of my father, to shield him from worry, but this time I couldn't hold back. For a while, we cried together, our tears bridging the distance, our silence more painful than words.

Then, unable to endure the weight of the moment any longer, I whispered, 'I'll be alright.'

My father's voice cracked with heartbreak, 'Just promise me that,' he replied. 'I'll be alright as long as you are.'

I wiped away my messy tears, and a small voice burst from the phone: my little sister Fatima, full of life.

'Sondos! We baked a cake! My birthday cake!'

Fatima sees every cake as her birthday cake. In her pure, sweet innocence, she truly believes she can celebrate her birthday whenever she wishes, as if the world still holds an endless reserve of joy, despite everything.

The happiness in her voice gave me strength. One is fortified by those one loves. Yesterday, Fatima was my remedy!

We began cleaning the lab, and at first, the task seemed impossible. My brother-in-law took on the heavy lifting, carrying broken furniture up to the school's rooftop, while Yasmeen and I scrubbed the floors and wiped down the shattered windows.

Most of the hard work fell to my sister, Raghda; she has a way of giving every task its full due. She took charge of fetching water, and afterwards she joined us in our cleaning, teasing us that we were far too slow for her liking.

As night fell, securing a private space for us women demanded a real sacrifice from Nael and his brothers. They spread their mats in front of the lab's entrance, and slept in the freezing cold without any means of heating, just so we could have a little shelter indoors.

I was exhausted to the point of collapse.

Yasmeen and I lay our mattresses next to one another, and the moment my head touched the pillow, a deep, aching sleep began to pull me under.

But Yasmeen, true to herself, believes bedtime chatter is a sacred ritual, one no circumstance should ever cancel, and just as I was about to sink into a beautiful rest, her voice pulled me back: 'Do you know what I'm craving?'

'What?' I mumbled, my voice thick with sleep.

'A spicy salad!'

'That's all? I thought you were going to say a lamb chop!'

'You're daft, you are! Where do you think we'd find even a handful of flour in times like these?'

I waved my hand dramatically: 'Abracadabra...boom! Yay, a spicy salad for Yasmeen, served fresh!'

Yasmeen burst into laughter.

I smothered my giggles with my hands, trying not to wake the others.

From the darkness came the grumpy voice of Umm Khaled, half-exhausted and half-scolding: 'Go to sleep, girls! No matter where we go, you lot are a nuisance!'

October 1, 2024

A DAY IN THE LIFE OF A WOMAN UNDER GENOCIDE

This morning, George Orwell's *1984* lingers in my thoughts.

'How does one man assert his power over another, Winston?'
'By making him suffer.'

These words feel awfully close to how Israel deals with Palestinians. Today is a new day, but we may as well be living in the past, dragged back a hundred years. If only that long-dead author could be my friend. Perhaps he would tell me about his life, about the details of his day. Perhaps he would know how to start a fire quickly, and what to do when it rained and the wood became too wet to burn?

I imagine channeling his physical strength — the size of his hands, the thickness of his skin — just for a few hours. My hands feel too fragile to light a fire, or endure its flames. Yet, after all that I've lived through, I fear that if I were to hold a rose in my hands, I would break its petals and ruin it.

I want to ask my long-dead author friend: How do the wild pigeons sound in the morning without the roar of fighter jets?

In the months since my last diary entry, I've been working with a youth initiative, providing psychological support for Gazan children. At noon, I travel to a school in Northern Gaza and spend time with the children of displaced families. For them, the word 'school' has been stripped of its original meaning; 'school', now, means nothing more than 'shelter'.

Today's mission is to gather the children in a circle and spark conversations to steer their thoughts away from war. In principle, this task seems simple. In practice, it's one of the hardest I've ever faced. Each child's story revolves around blood, loss and destruction. I try asking about their dreams for the future. But every time a child answers, they start with, 'When the war ends...'

One little girl, Masa, is particularly dear to my heart. Her name means 'precious gem'. She's five years old, and is convinced that, when the war ends, her father will return. Together, they'll play with her toys on her colourful bed, and she'll scold him for being away so long. But Masa's father isn't coming back; he's been lost to the war, along with her home and her bed.

I hug her and kiss her. We sit together in the middle of the circle. I ask the other children to share the things they love most about Masa and give her high fives. I can't help but feel the weight of their words.

After work, my colleague Noor and I decide to go to the market. Much like 'school', the word 'market' has lost most of its meaning. Supplies are scarce, prices are high and most of the food is canned.

A doctor has told Noor that her son is malnourished. She points to the shelves of cans and says, 'Do they expect these to provide my children with the nutrients they need to grow? This food is just meant to fill their bellies, nothing more. The bodies of adults are already exhausted; imagine the effect on a child!'

At night, the children's stories fill my thoughts. So many stories have accumulated, I'm afraid I might forget them. My mind can't keep pace with everything we've lived through, every detail of this genocide. Each time I try to craft a narrative, a new story is born, and I try to shape that one too. My words have become clumsy and tangled. My thoughts appear in half-formed sentences, splintered by the overwhelming things I've seen and experienced.

As I lay my head on the pillow, after almost a year of this genocide, I realise how disappointed I've become. How much I've let others down. How deeply sad I am.

I don't know who to share these feelings with. I don't know how to wave at someone and say, 'Hello, there's a massive fire inside me. Do you think you could help put it out?'

I feel alone with all these little details, and alone with all the big ones.

WHEN MEMORY BECOMES CONSOLATION

I feel like I'm walking on a taut thread, balancing in mid-air. I haven't adapted to the harsh way of life imposed on us. I refuse to adapt to this.

Instead, I revisit old photos and whisper to myself, 'This is who I am: a butterfly, fluttering lightly. I won't let sorrow turn me into a mountain, weighed down by despair. I know my steps have become heavier, and the stabs of betrayal deeper, but from the depths of my heart, I refuse to let scenes of our slaughter become routine. I refuse to let the souls of my friends and loved ones disappear into passing numbers on news broadcasts, I refuse for our name, as Palestinians, to be synonymous with only misery and despair.'

Today is Thursday, and for the umpteenth day in a row, Israel maintains the closure of the Kerem Shalom Crossing: the lifeline that keeps our food markets and our healthcare going. Hospitals in Gaza face severe shortages of medicine and fuel. Israeli bombing continues in many different neighbourhoods.

Here, in the North, food is scarce and prices have skyrocketed. The Israeli strategy of starvation has continued for over a year now, and no international law or humanitarian plea seems capable of stopping it.

What a farce this world is.

On my way to work today, I see a blonde-haired little girl who looks just like Fatima. I stop, hug her and almost kiss her before catching and chiding myself: *She's not your sister; it's just longing you're feeling.*

As I reach the school, a missile lands near the market next door. The screams of mothers fill the air as they run to find their children. I realise that venturing outside is not a safe thing to do, but working with the children and trying to ease their suffering lifts some of the weight from my shoulders. Nevertheless, today's missile incident causes all of our lessons to be postponed in much the same way everything else has been postponed since the start of this genocide. Life itself is on hold until further notice.

In Gaza, under such brutality, you find yourself struggling to remember that you're human; that you deserve life. Israel gives you nothing to help you recall this fact: not a sip of drinkable water, not even a warm shower to wash off the dust of war.

From Day One of this genocide, the Israelis announced loud and clear: 'No water, no food, no electricity.' And for seventeen years before that, they imposed a suffocating blockade on us, making us feel as though even the air we breathed was being monitored and rationed.[11] A world busy with its own news and gossip had forgotten that there were human beings with hearts and blood in Gaza, and only woke up on October 7, shocked, as if nothing had happened before that date, and suddenly concluded that we were beyond the salvation of 'international' or 'humanitarian' law.

The sting of memory is painful, yet essential to our survival, dear reader. Once, we had lives. We had friends. We had Gaza, with its sea, with its bright, breezy mornings, with its balmy evenings which still reside inside us, strong and defiant against forgetfulness. I remember poetry: I loved it and still do. I remember my dreams and ambitions which I will one day nurture again and see grow. I remember my breakfast in the Islamic University courtyard, the sound of car horns in the morning traffic and the writing I've left unfinished.

I remember that I remember!

They want to amputate my memory. They want to erase every trace of that life.

But still, I remember.

I remember Gaza as it was: its streets full of life, the little shop on the corner whose owner would expertly fry falafel, its smell stirring the birds in my stomach.

I remember that I remember, and I will not have that memory erased.

Israel wants to strip me of my humanity. But I always remind myself that I am a spirit, a beating heart, a free being. They don't want me to see myself as anything but a number, a voiceless creature. And when they declared, 'No water, no food, no electricity,' it's as if they were also whispering, from the corners of their mouths, 'No memory, no humanity.'

But they have failed.

I think, I write, and I remember.

I remember that I remember, and I will not have that memory erased.

I remember the day I was forced by their cruelty to eat animal feed; there was no flour, and the feed's rough surface tore the roof of my mouth. I remember them dragging the men from our neighbourhood along the street, barefoot and naked before our eyes. I remember how my sister's children lay dead, unburied, for days.

In the worst moments, I turned inward, I began to write. And writing became my salvation. Every tyrant on earth has tried to control the oppressed, depriving them of the simplest necessities of life, but none has ever succeeded in controlling their thoughts. Thoughts escape shackles. Thoughts soar into the skies of freedom.

Yes, I remember.

I remember that I remember, and I will not have that memory erased.

I once had a life. I once had a home. I once had a family who wrapped me in warmth. In this age of injustice, it feels as though we're living in the days of Abu Talib's boycott,[12] hoping for a noble spirit to tear up the 'document' and end the hunger gnawing at our children's bellies. But I have my memory, I have my pen and I have the world.

I remember that I remember.

I will not have that memory erased.

December 19, 2024

FINDING JOY IN THE RAIN

The voices of the displaced women pull me from my thoughts. These women sit on the roadside, seeking the warmth of the sun. They wear colourful prayer gowns while their children dance around them, bundled in heavy coats. I've often observed them from my window, watching them follow the sun as it shifts direction, only returning to their tents at nightfall—tents which barely offer protection from the biting cold of winter nights. These are the newly displaced: people who have fled their homes in the Far North of the Strip and found refuge in a school playground. Others have pitched their tents on farmland or in hospital courtyards. The designated shelters have already overflowed with arrivals.

Today, as I walk past this crowded camp of tents, I catch a glimpse of a familiar face, a face time hasn't entirely erased, despite everything.

Hesitant, I approach. When our eyes meet, I realise it's Maram: an old friend from school. Her features are etched with exhaustion and shock; she doesn't recognise me, at least not at first.

I introduce myself, and mention some mutual friends who once shared our classroom laughter. Only then does her expression soften, as though she is returning to the present.

'You've changed so much since school,' she says.

Cautiously, I ask how she ended up here.

Maram lets out a deep sigh, releasing years of pain in one breath. 'It's only been a week, or maybe a little more. We escaped Jabalia Camp by some miracle. We thought we wouldn't make it. The airstrikes were relentless. Shells were falling randomly, destroying people's homes.'

I look at her face, marked by the scars of war and displacement.

'We tried to stay in Jabalia until the very last moment. We thought things might calm down. But the Israeli soldiers stormed our neighbourhood, arresting all the men and forcing the women and children out of their homes. We had nowhere to go, so this is where we ended up.'

She gestures to a nearby tent, barely large enough to shelter the weary bodies of her children and her husband's family.

In a tone that blends resignation and bitterness, she says, 'This is our home now.'

With shaking hands, she pulls her phone from her bag and scrolls through an album filled with images circulating on social media: many show vast areas of Jabalia reduced to rubble, total destruction that leaves no hope for return. She pauses on a different picture, her trembling voice barely audible, as if it might shatter in the air: 'This was *our* home. Do you remember it? You visited me there on my eighteenth birthday.'

The memory surfaces like a scene from another life. I had forgotten Maram's birthday until the last minute, and had to quickly prepare a gift: wrapping a journal in pink ribbon. Maram was an exceptional student, her fashion coordination was striking. On the day of her party, I discovered the secret behind Maram's elegance: her mother, who was very attentive to the smallest of details.

As a souvenir of her daughter's birthday, Maram's mother gave us all beautiful red pens — a lovely gesture. Later, Maram fell in love with a young man from Jabalia Camp. Her family rejected this pairing due to the man's living situation as a refugee[13] and the fact that he shared a small house with his family. But despite these challenges, their love story won out: they got married, received her family's acceptance and overcame the obstacles society placed in their way.

71

Now, they are here: living in a tent.

'Yes,' I tell Maram, 'I remember your birthday.'

What more can I add? Words seem futile. So I look at Maram in silence, tears welling in my eyes. Standing by her side is the only thing I can offer, though we both know it isn't enough. Together, we stare at the tent that has become her home. I find myself wondering: how much strength does it take for a person to remain standing amidst such devastation?

December 21, 2024

THE DEFERRED TOMORROW

The people here live on hope and hope alone.

In the gatherings held by the sides of tents, there is no talk except about the progress of negotiations and the chance of returning to homes. Something in our eyes hints at anticipation. And in our chests: a deep fear.

Negotiations seem to be advancing, and a ceasefire might be imminent, or so the leaks from Hebrew media suggest. But we always pay the price for negotiations with blood. New invasions, intense bombing and more casualties: this is what Israel calls 'military pressure' against the resistance. As I write, Kamal Adwan Hospital in Beit Lahia is under siege; doctors and patients are living through days of fear and hunger. The hospital's director, Dr. Hussam Abu Safiya,[14] issued a call to the World Health Organisation and all humanitarian organisations, asking for fuel to be delivered, but his call went unanswered. Today, his demands had been humbled: he only asked for food and water for the patients and medical staff.

Will anyone respond? I doubt it.

Each of us prepares for the aftermath of war in their own way. I plan to bring some green back to our balcony with peas, radishes, parsley and garlic. I wish I could plant roses and carnations, but the seeds we have available dictate the fate of our gardens. My father, with his loving spirit, calls to tell me he will bring me hazelnut chocolate and hot drinks when he returns from the displacement camp in the South. Our neighbour is also working non-stop: removing the rubble piled in front of his house, sealing the broken windows with plastic sheeting and preparing to welcome his grandchildren home.

On the other side, an Israeli minister talks about the need for a Jewish settlement in Gaza and declares that she will be the first to build a house here. I hope this is nothing more than a threat, but if Israel occupies Gaza again and builds settlements on its land, will they repeat their infamous lie: 'A land without a people for a people without a land?' Or is that lie too old-fashioned? Will they invent a new lie to replace it?

My cousin Iman visits and suggests we go to the market. After an interruption of nine long months, the stalls have seen a sudden influx of fruit and vegetables. Sometimes we laugh at our situation, and joke with each other: 'Do you remember what meat is? Do you remember how watermelon tastes?'

Before the war, the heart of trade in Gaza was along Omar al-Mukhtar Street, through al-Rimal neighbourhood and up to Palestine Square, where activity and noise continued into the late hours of night. Today, al-Rimal is a heap of rubble, deserted by all but a few families. If you scream there, your voice will echo back to you. At night, no one dares to leave their home; Israeli drones fly incessantly, and the sounds of barking dogs and screaming children spread fear into every corner.

In place of al-Rimal, the old al-Daraj neighbourhood has become our shopping centre, with wooden stalls and animal-drawn carts filling the streets. The road here is blocked by rubble from a bombed house. So, to reach the market, we have to cross an agricultural area which has been turned into a mass grave. This area, about 500 square metres, holds the bodies of those killed between December 5-8, 2023. The gravestones bear no individual names, only the names of families. The first is for the Shobaki family, holding five bodies. The second is for the Hassan family, holding eleven bodies. Some are marked 'unknown.' We recite the Fatiha prayer for the martyrs, and continue on our way.

At the market, we look at the fruits as if they are Eid sweets; I wish I could kiss every tomato on its cheeks. We buy apples, bananas and lemons, and I take a picture of a stall filled with vibrant colours; I've grown tired of the colour grey.

Finally, we reach my uncle Mohammed's house, our arms laden with treasures. My little cousin, born in January, during the height of the war, is named 'Salam', in the hope she may receive a share of the peace her name represents. Salam has never tasted formula milk or baby food. The first word Salam uttered was 'adas,' meaning 'lentils', not because it is an easy word to pronounce in Arabic, but because lentils have been her main source of food for a long time. Today, words like 'apple' and 'banana' are entering Salam's vocabulary for the first time. But after tasting her first banana, Salam refuses to accept it, as if the taste of lentils is truly closer to her heart. Her four-year-old sister, Maryam, even tries to eat a banana with its peel intact. It seems we will have to teach our children the basics of eating fruit all over again — we, the people of agriculture!

January 2, 2025

WHAT IF, ON A RAINY NIGHT, YOUR CEILING WERE THE SKY?

It's raining, and I've come to hate rainy mornings.

With every drop that falls, my heart breaks for the people living in tents. My father is one of them. I call to check on him and ask how he spent the night. His voice sounds weak, showing symptoms of a winter cold. He tells me water leaked under the tent last night, soaking his belongings and preventing him and my younger siblings from sleeping.

My father — my 'heart's master', as I have always called him — was always full of tenderness and care for us at home. During the long winter nights of childhood, my father moved between his children like a bustling bee, making sure we were safe and warm, protecting us from the cold, ensuring the windows and doors were tightly shut and sealing any crack that might let a breeze in. I capture this image in my mind before it can slip into the depths of my memory.

Whenever my father asks with deep concern about me and our family in the North, I want to reply: 'Father, don't worry. My heart is warm and reassured because of you.'

This afternoon, I'm working with a volunteer team in al-Yarmouk area of Gaza City. Tents are scattered along the sides of the road in a haphazard manner, stretching more than a mile between the municipal library and al-Wahda Junction.

Near al-Wafa Hospital, there's a more organised tent settlement, known as al-Wafa Camp, whose management assist us as we begin distributing blankets and covering tents with waterproof tarpaulins. This camp alone houses 80 families, including the Kilani, Attatra and Sobeh families, mostly displaced from the northern city of Beit Lahia.

Before the war, Beit Lahia was famous for its fertile lands and thriving agriculture. It was especially well-known for its strawberries, which the locals described as 'red gold.' These strawberries were exported worldwide, while the area's citrus fruits, grapes and guavas contributed significantly to the local economy. Now, these beautiful farmlands have been all but wiped out by the Israeli soldiers stationed there.

Still, I am struck by the beauty of Beit Lahia's displaced children. Some have long braids, others have blonde hair and coloured eyes. I find myself saying to the camp manager: 'I think one of the conditions for joining the camp is having beautiful children.'

One of these children looks at me sharply, and says, 'Why didn't you give me a blanket?'

'Don't worry, sweetie, come with me. If there are any extra blankets, I'll give you one.'

She grabs my hand, and we head to the administration tent at the front of the camp, from which the camp's affairs are managed. But we can't find any blankets so, instead, I offer her a sweet. She accepts it reluctantly.

Abu Anas, an 80-year-old man, who left his house in Beit Lahia under a barrage of Israeli fire, tells me: 'Life is in God's hands. I don't have much time left. A day, a month, or even a year — it doesn't make much difference to me. But my children are still young. I carry their fate on my shoulders, and I fear they would have been arrested or killed in their prime if we'd stayed. That's why we left.'

He adds: 'My son Anas is an exceptional engineering student, top of his class, and I want him to graduate. We left our house with only the things we could carry. But my wife has sold her gold bracelets to buy our son a laptop so he can continue his studies.'

Abu Anas tells me that the memory of sitting in his orchard, on his own land, under the wild mulberry trees, meant everything to him. He had cultivated strawberries on that land for more than twenty years. At the end of our conversation, he embraces me with sincere prayers and a faith that reminds me of my father's.

After a long and exhausting day, I am greeted by my new cat, Ghandora, adopted from one of my sister's neighbours who could no longer afford to feed her. The price of dry food has reached 300 Shekels, almost 90 British pounds, for a 1kg bag which lasts Ghandora four days. Ghandora circles me and tries to cling to my trousers. I lift her into my arms, recharging myself with her love and affection. 'Ghandora', in Arabic, means 'to walk with pride and grace.'

I turn on the radio. The heavy rains have flooded over 1,500 tents.

January 19, 2025

TEARS SHED, LIFE REKINDLED

My heart, once weary and sceptical, finds itself embracing hope again. Today, the ceasefire, brokered by Qatar, Egypt and the US, comes into effect, after a fourteen-month inferno which has claimed the lives of more than 60,000 martyrs and missing persons, witnessed over 10,000 separate massacres, displaced more than two million people and robbed 18,000 children of life before they could even begin to live it.

I have to remember the figures: 1,600 families wiped out entirely, struck off the registry of life. The population of Gaza has fallen by six per cent. Tens of thousands of injured people lie groaning in pain, without access to hospitals. Thousands remain in Israeli detention, or simply missing, their fate unknown.

This war has reached into every home in Gaza, touching every family, scarring every heart. It has reduced our city to rubble, unfit for people. We've lived through days which felt like an endless nightmare. Bodies fell, limbs were torn off, survival seemed impossible. Every conceivable form of death has been visited upon us. At times, I even found myself wishing for death as a merciful escape.

Yet today marks the beginning of a transition from screaming to prolonged mourning. I weep for my sisters' martyred children — Randa has lost four children and a grandchild; Umm Arafrah has lost her son, Ahmad — I cry for each of them, one by one.

I mourn the irreplaceable loss of the finest minds of our community: thinkers, doctors, writers and influencers. What a monumental tragedy it is to face such calculated destruction, a genocide designed with malicious precision to strip away the backbone of our society, across every field of life. If there is any victory, it has come at the steepest of prices: every drop of our blood until the very last moment.

In the coming week, the Northern Gaza Valley will witness two heart-wrenching tasks: the recovery of the bodies of loved ones buried beneath the rubble and the agonising search for those who are missing.

But amid all of this sorrow, the enduring spirit of our people will shine. Many will work tirelessly to prepare the remaining homes and shelters, ready to welcome home the displaced. For many of those returning to the North, life in a tent will become the new reality. The restoration of what can be salvaged will demand a collective effort, with neighbours opening their doors to one another, offering whatever space we have left. This will culminate in a flood of tears as people return to their lands, crossing the Netzarim Corridor [a military corridor which divides the Gaza Strip, imposed by the Israelis during the genocide] to embrace their loved ones and the land they call home. And with the release of the first prisoners from the occupation's prisons, especially the world's longest-serving political prisoner, Nael Barghouti,[15] there will be a flicker of light. Barghouti himself said, 'I've witnessed the prison gates change twice during my captivity. The iron rusted, but our spirits never corroded.'

We will bring our children back to the schools, they have been deprived of education for far too long. We will give them hope for a bright future. We will rebuild our mosques and churches, places that have always been beacons of tolerance. This will be a time for healing, for self-reflection and for learning from our past mistakes. It will also be a time to move towards a united national path.

Today, the Palestinian people deserve the support of the entire world. We need outstretched hands, careful reflection and collective action to plan for a future that grants our children their right to a better life. We know how to persevere and live with dignity, but today we need the world's support to build a better tomorrow, where hope triumphs and peace becomes our reality.

The laughter of children will return. The hearts of bereaved mothers will find solace. Fear will no longer haunt us. We long for the silence of the guns and the drones. We yearn for the voice of peace to rise above it all.

January 23, 2025

WAR-FREE MORNING, HAUNTED BY ITS LEGACY

Am I actually awake? Can this really be the way mornings are now: without the roar of planes or the crackle of gunfire?

Today is the fifth day since the ceasefire was declared. An eerie silence fills the void that was once charged with anxiety — a silence so loud it feels as if the morning is testing us. Can we really adapt to peace, this new condition? Can we make it our home again?

After a year and a half of separation, I will soon embrace my father and my siblings. I imagine our reunion: an embrace full of yearning in which the laughter of restoration will mix with the tears of loss for what has passed.

Early in the morning, I go to the UNRWA office to update my family's record. The queue is long, stretching like a heavy shadow across time, bearing the burden of all the waiting that has persisted since 1948. The faces of those around me are pale and weighed down. But their eyes show a glimmer of hope among the devastation. In a soft voice, tinged with sadness, the lady beside me begins to share her story.

'My family fled Gaza City,' she explains. 'My father, my brothers and their children: fifteen people left together. But now, when they return, there will only be nine.' She pauses briefly, trying to gather her words, which fall heavily with the weight of her sorrow, 'I still can't accept that they're gone forever. Sometimes, I go into their rooms. I look at their possessions and I feel as if they'll return at any moment. My heart breaks every time. How did they leave like this? How did they go without saying goodbye?'

I feel her pain intertwine with mine. The sorrow here isn't individual, but collective: a grief shared by every home in Gaza.

A young man catches my attention. He is handing out cups of hot coffee, free of charge. He smiles and says simply, 'This is my gift to you. We may wait a long time, but at least we'll be warm.'

The lady beside me takes one of his cups, then turns back to me. 'Despite all this pain,' she says, 'we still find among us those who bring gestures like this. Gaza is not just what the war has destroyed, Gaza is the people who remind us every day that goodness still exists.'

When I return home, I find guests have gathered to help my sister Shireen's neighbours retrieve the body of their daughter, Daila, who has been buried in my sister's yard in the Sheikh Radwan neighbourhood for many months. The story goes back to the early days of the invasion, when young Daila and several others sought refuge in my sister's home, fleeing the Israeli tanks. Amid the heavy bombardment and the news of bodies falling in the streets, the young woman's heart suddenly gave in. Her pregnant body couldn't withstand the terror.

There had been no time or place to bury her properly. With the help of neighbours, she was buried in my sister's yard. Shortly afterwards, my sister's house was completely bombed. Now, after months, her family is trying to recover her body and bury her with dignity. I look at the simple tools they have brought with them. I wonder: can these tools withstand all this rubble? Or will the tragedy of Daila remain a testament to all that can't be recovered?

January 25, 2025

ISRAEL HASN'T DECIDED IF WE'LL MEET

This morning, news spreads that Israel has allowed the opening of the Netzarim Checkpoint, and hundreds of thousands of displaced Palestinians are getting ready to return to their homes. I can't contain my joy. I put on my clothes and rush to the seafront, to al-Rasheed Road. I wouldn't be late for my father, not even by a minute.

I join a crowd of people, all like myself. Beside me stands Sharifa, my neighbour, who has been separated from her children throughout the war. Around us: mothers, fathers, sisters, lovers and friends. Everyone gathers, longing for the embrace that will calm their hearts.

Time drags on. Our excitement fades under the scorching sun. A rumour begins to circulate: the opening of the checkpoint has been postponed. Soon, it becomes clear that this isn't a rumour, it's the bitter truth.

Sharifa and I walk home in silence, our silence mirroring the depth of our disappointment.

When I open the door, my sister Saja asks me, 'What happened?'

'Israel hasn't decided whether we can meet yet,' I reply.

I think I will sleep for a long time tonight, taking my revenge on everything by refusing to wake.

January 27, 2025

AT ROUNDABOUT SEVENTEEN

Finally, Israel has opened the Netzarim Checkpoint and the return of the displaced has begun in large numbers. Today, the

crowds are overwhelming: men, women and children are shouting 'Allahu Akbar' over and over again, their cries blend into a
powerful chant. It looks like a scene from the Day of Judgement.

At this very moment, my father is walking to reach me. His
health isn't perfect, and I worry about the distance, but he is
determined not to wait for the vehicles at the Salah al-Din
checkpoint. Like most of the displaced people, he has chosen
to walk.[16]

With my father is Fatima, now five years old, and Mahmoud,
now eight. Because of the crowds, my father has written their
names and his contact number on their arms. He will, of
course, hold their hands tightly throughout. They are carrying
nothing but water bottles and dates.

I've agreed to meet them all here, at Roundabout Seventeen,
the nearest place to the checkpoint that taxis are allowed to
reach. I've tried to contact my father repeatedly, but the signal
is patchy. Eventually my phone rings, and my father tells me
they've been delayed by two hours.

I sit with a former classmate and her mother on the roof of their
building, overlooking al-Rasheed Road and witnessing the
return of so many Gazans to their homes in the North. It's a
historic and legendary sight: the first time such a scene of return
has occurred in the history of the Palestinian displacement.
People's fears of being forced outside the borders of Palestine
are gone. But, as far as the eye can see, Gaza looks like a desert.
Our people are returning to a land devoid of life. Even the
sewage systems and street lights have been uprooted by Israeli
bulldozers.

Al-Rasheed was once one of Gaza's busiest streets, famous
for the wedding halls and towering buildings, which ran along
the coast, always buzzing with people. It had diverse architec-
ture: luxurious hotels on its eastern side, and youthful cafés on

its western side — cafés which stayed open long into the night. Before the genocide, the street had offered an escape from the reality of the seventeen-year siege and the mass unemployment it caused. Despite the crises Gaza endured, the crowded cafés and modern cars made al-Rasheed Street feel like a space for life: a living testament to Palestinian resilience.

Now, Israel's war machine has turned the street into a pile of rubble. Heavy bombing has destroyed its landmarks, wiping out its vibrant pulse. Large crowds are gazing around in shock at the scale of destruction, astonishment and fear clearly written on their faces.

Many keep repeating, 'Everything is perishable, but the face of your Lord, full of majesty and honour, will remain.'[17]

I receive a message from my father; he's close to the round-about. It's afternoon now, and the atmosphere is at its peak. The traffic is unbearable, and my heart races with every moment, quickening as the meeting draws closer.

At first I see him from a distance. For a moment, I can't believe my eyes. It feels as though my heart has forgotten how to beat. Is this really my father? But his features, his stance and that aura: I can't be mistaken.

Suddenly, I realise I'm not dreaming. I scream with all my heart, 'Father! There's my father!'

I run towards him as if I'm flying, as though the wind is pushing me with a force I've never known. The closer I get, the more my voice trembles.

'Yes, it's my father! It's my father! It's my father!'

I feel like the whole world has collapsed into the tiny space between us. I want to be in his arms in the blink of an eye. If I wait even a moment longer, I feel he might disappear, or someone might take him from me.

I throw myself into his embrace. He holds me tightly, and

kisses my forehead. I hold his hand and kiss it. Then, I look into his eyes and find them filled with tears — tears I have never seen him shed before. I wipe them away and he wipes away mine. I kiss his cheeks, once, twice, a hundred times.

My father's hug in this vast world is my paradise. But war has changed us, and my father has changed the most. He has grown older, withered. His body has become thin, his eyes dull. I almost can't comprehend this image of him.

There's a picture imprinted in my mind, a picture I never want to replace: my father, strong, with a well-groomed beard, traditional robe, keffiyeh and commanding presence. In this picture he sits, one foot over the other, holding a book in his hand, his loud voice filling the air at a lecture or a gathering.

Weakness doesn't suit my father. My father is strong.

March 19, 2025

CHASED BY WAR, STARVED BY SIEGE, FORGOTTEN BY THE WORLD

I feel like a drowning man who reaches the surface, gasping for air, only to be dragged down again by another whirlpool, leaving him suspended between life and death, with no ground beneath his feet, and no horizon for salvation.

After a ceasefire that lasted only eight weeks and two days, war has returned, overturning everything we've desperately tried to hold on to. Before today, I made a forced truce with our circumstances, accepting life as it is, despite the absence of basic necessities and the abundance of suffering. In my mind, I painted visions of a future filled with peace, of cities without shelling, of days without mourning. But our wounds have not yet healed. We have not buried our dead. We have not cleared the rubble. We have not even grasped what has happened to us, let alone what is still happening.

At 2am, we were preparing suhoor [the pre-dawn meal Muslims eat before fasting during Ramadan] when, suddenly, intense streaks of fire shook the walls of the house, the sound of death shattering our silence.

My sister Fatima screamed in terror, 'The missile is coming back for us again! Sondos, tell it to go away! Please!'

Trying to calm her, I played along, my shaking voice betraying me, 'Get away from Fatoum, you wicked missile!'

At dawn, we gather to pray. My father recites, 'And We will surely test you with something of fear and hunger and a loss of wealth and lives and fruits, but give good tidings to the patient.'[18]

I weep.

The light of day brings no hope, only grim numbers: more than 300 martyrs, dozens wounded and waves of displaced families flooding the streets of Northern and Eastern Gaza.[19] Thousands are being forced to flee again, carrying their homes on their backs, searching for shelter where none exists. Children will be crying, exhausted from the long walk. Mothers will desperately try to soothe them, stricken with fear. Fathers will drag their weary steps under the blazing sun, lost with no destination.

Israel does not stop at killing; it hunts sorrow itself, targeting grief before tears can dry. In Beit Lahia, its missiles struck a mourning tent in al-Salateen neighbourhood, turning it into a mass grave, and creating 50 martyrs in an instant.

What kind of cruelty kills grief twice? What kind of crime targets tears before they even dry?

I don't want to lose another loved one. I haven't recovered from the loss of my sisters' children. I can't endure another famine. My heart is devoured, screaming for a moment of safety. The trial is immense, O God. We do not object to your decree, but we are exhausted.

To the world I say: do not let Israel kill me this time.
Do something, anything, please!
I want to live.

NOTES

1. Fadwa Tuqan: Prominent poet of Palestinian resistance, her work often detailed the hardship of life under Israeli occupation. Tuqan died in 2003, during the Second Intifada, at the age of 86.

2. On December 17, 2023, fewer than two months after this diary entry was written, the YMCA in Gaza City was destroyed by Israeli bombing.

3. Although gunpowder as a substance is no longer commonly used, '*baroud*', the Arabic word for gunpowder, remains popular amongst Gazans when describing the smell of gunfire and explosives.

4. The IDF (Israeli Defense Forces) deploy white phosphorous in felt-soaked wedges which burn at 815 degrees Celsius and cause severe, often fatal burns; in many cases burning through skin, muscle and bone. Fragments of white phosphorus can remain in a wound and later reignite when exposed to oxygen. Chemical side effects of white phosphorous on the human body include muscle damage and kidney failure, sometimes resulting in lifelong pain or death.

5. According to UNRWA (the United Nations Relief and Works Agency for Palestine Refugees in the Near East), the IDF attack on al-Fakhoura School in Jabalia Refugee Camp on January 6, 2009 killed over 40 Palestinians. Just eleven days later, Iyad al-Baba, a Palestinian photographer working for UNRWA, captured photographic evidence of a similar white phosphorous attack on another UNRWA school in nearby Beit Lahia. In the aftermath of these assaults, Amnesty International reported, 'hundreds of white phosphorus-impregnated wedges in residential areas all over Gaza, still smouldering weeks after they had been fired'. Al-Fakhoura School itself was again the target of several airstrikes during Israel's heavy bombardment of the Jabalia Refugee Camp on November 17-18, 2023, killing over 60 Palestinians, as reported by Al Jazeera.

6. Ghassan Kanafani: Giant of Palestinian literature, whose many novels include *Men in the Sun* (1962) and *Return to Haifa* (1970). As a child, Kanafani and his family were forcibly displaced from their home in Historic Palestine by Zionist militias. He later became the spokesman of the PFLP (Popular Front for the Liberation of Palestine). Kanafani was murdered by an Israeli car bomb in 1972, alongside his seventeen-year-old niece.

7. Sondos refers to her eldest sister Rajaa by her kunya, Umm Arafah. A kunya is an honorific derived from the name of a person's eldest child. In this case Umm Arafah is the mother of Arafah, just as Abu Sami is the father of Sami. The use of a kunya often denotes respect for a person's age and status.

8. During the forced displacement on October 13, an Israeli airstrike killed 70 civilians on Salah al-Din Road as they followed orders to evacuate to Southern Gaza. Videos documenting the aftermath of the strike, verified by the BBC, show the bodies of men, women and children. The shocking violence of this attack is also mentioned in Nahil and Ala'a's diary entries for October 13, 2023.

9. Israel's remote-controlled quadcopter drones are capable of surveillance, gunfire and 'suicide' bomb attacks. They are also frequently used as an instrument of psychological warfare: their loud and near-constant whine disrupting sleep and signalling the ever-present threat of violence; their speakers used to play recordings of screaming women and children in order to draw Palestinians into the streets before firing on them. In August 2024, ten months into the genocide, the Palestinian Health Ministry in Gaza reported that approximately 500 men, 350 women and 150 children had been killed by quadcopter drones. Dr Nabeel Rana, an American surgeon who volunteered in Gaza in 2024, has described a high number of incidents in which quadcopters targeted the genitals of young Palestinian men, telling *Mother Jones* that '[patients] would come in with no other injuries, and would lose their testicles. They're healthy young men, but they'll never have kids. Either [the drone pilots] are trying to decimate the future of a society, or it's just sick entertainment. And I don't know which one it is'.

10. Tamim al-Barghouti: Palestinian-Egyptian poet and journalist. A well-known supporter of Palestinian liberation.

11. In 2007, Israel imposed a blockade on the Gaza Strip: destroying Gaza's ability to trade internationally, controlling Gaza's borders, restricting the free movement of people and segregating Palestinians in Gaza from Palestinians in the West Bank and Historic Palestine. The resulting description of the Gaza Strip as 'an open-air prison', has been used by many Palestinians as well as the international organisations Human Rights Watch and the Norwegian Refugee Council.

12. A reference to early Islamic history. The document in question was an agreement between leaders of the Quraysh Tribe, imposing a trade and marriage boycott against supporters of the Islamic prophet Muhammad.

13. Here, a common distinction is made. The term 'refugee' is used to describe a family with roots in Historic Palestine, who have been displaced into Gaza from another part of the homeland. The term 'displaced person', is used to describe those who have been internally displaced during the genocide. Jabalia Refugee Camp was founded in 1948, to shelter those displaced during the Nakba. The camp is distinct from, but adjacent to, the city of Jabalia.

14. Dr Hussam Abu Safiya: Medical director of Kamal Adwan Hospital in Beit Lahia from February to December 2024. Despite multiple attacks on his hospital, the murder of his fifteen-year-old son by Israeli forces and serious injuries sustained from a drone strike, Dr Abu Safiya and his staff refused to abandon patients at what had become (as a product of Israeli aggression against Gazan hospitals) the only functioning hospital in North Gaza. On December 27, 2024, Dr Abu Safiya was abducted by Israeli Forces from Kamal Adwan during an assault on the hospital. He was initially held in Israel's infamous Sde Teiman military detention camp, before being transferred to Ofer Prison where, according to Samir al-Mana'ama, a lawyer with the Al Mezan Center for Human Rights, Dr Safiya was held in solitary confinement for 25 days, and subjected to continuous interrogation, includ-

ing torture. At the time of publication, he remains in Israeli detention.

15. Al-Barghouti was imprisoned from 1978-2011, and again from 2014-2025. He was released on February 27, 2025, nine days after this diary entry was written.

16. Displaced people were allowed to return to the North of the Strip on foot, via al-Rasheed Road, without being checked. Vehicles were allowed to return via Salah al-Din Road, but were subject to checks carried out under Egyptian and Qatari supervision.

17. Verse 55:27 of *The Quran*. From the Surah Ar-Rahman: 'The Merciful'.

18. Verse 2:155 of *The Quran*. From the Surah al-Baqarah: 'The Cow'.

19. The death toll from Israel's ceasefire-breaking assault later rose to over 400 dead and over 550 injured.

Nahil Mohana

NAHIL MOHANA is the author of the novel *No Men Allowed*, the short story collection *Life in a Square Metre* and six plays including *High Pressure*, which received the 2008 Abdul Mohsin Al-Qattan Prize; *Ghoson*, which received the 2008 Children's Culture Award; and *Lipstick*, which was produced by the Royal Court Theatre, London. Her writing has appeared in *AGNI Online*, *Literary Hub*, and *The Washington Post*. Extracts from her diaries have been performed by Maxine Peake at the Barbican Theatre, London, and Julie-Yara Atz at the Belgrade Theatre, Coventry.

To Iman,
How I wish I had been with you at the time of your
martydom. Were you in such a hurry to leave?

TODAY, I WOKE TO the sound of successive raids in the skies over Gaza. They were strange and terrifying sounds, especially to those of us who live in the northern region of the Strip, the most dangerous area to live, where there are large expanses of land from which resistance missiles are often launched, and which Israel often attacks in turn.

Today was supposed to be the seventh day of what's come to be known as 'Pink Month': a series of events designed to promote breast cancer awareness and early detection. Earlier in the week, cultural centres in Gaza and Ramallah were simultaneously illuminated in pink — making us feel that we are all members of one Palestinian nation — and I was among the spectators of a silent theatrical performance in Gaza City, dedicated to the occasion. All those doctors and health campaigners in attendance couldn't have guessed that there would soon be 99 issues more urgent than the early detection of breast cancer; the first and foremost of which is the safety of our children.

For most of this morning, we thought the noise was just an escalation: the kind of clash we had become accustomed to since the 2014 war, which lasted more than fifty days. We assumed the bombing would pass like a storm, that calm would soon return to the skies above Gaza.

But, my friend, we were wrong.

We all felt shock, yesterday, when we saw the television news footage of resistance soldiers entering Israeli territories and kidnapping high-ranking IDF officials, among others, and detaining them. But our initial surprise and sense of vengeance, for decades of slaughter, quickly dissipated as we realised how much this was going to cost us.

After the announcement that hostages had been taken, the Israeli bombardment began to intensify. Suddenly, the power was cut off. Minutes later, internet services were cut too. Telecommunication companies began sending text messages to customers, stating that there were problems in the networks due to the airstrikes, that they would work to fix them as soon as possible. I lost contact with all my friends abroad and at home. A sense of immense dread started to sink in. The situation was unprecedented.

Today, all schools have been suspended: a decision from the Ministry of Education. I cannot find words to reassure Habiba, my twelve-year-old daughter. I'm surprised how sophisticated and complex her questions are. Back in 2021, during the last onslaught, Habiba was younger and easier to lie to. In the 2014 war, I even told her that the explosions were just doors slamming loudly further down the street. I spent that summer distracting her with crisps, Kinder Eggs and cartoons on my tablet, the volume turned up to drown out the distant bombing. I couldn't believe I was openly lying to my child.

But now, lying is pointless. Habiba picks up words from the radio and those around her. Words like 'resistance', 'Hamas', 'hostages' and 'Sederot'. She comes to ask me what they mean. Explaining is going to be extremely tricky.

October 9, 2023

The electricity generator in our house only works for one hour a day due to a shortage of diesel. This means we have only one hour to get everything done: cooking, talking with friends on the phone, household chores, showering (a pump is needed to get water to the building) and watching the television news.

Outside, the Israeli shelling continues, ever more intense and brutal. Until now, we really believed civilians were exempt from this brutality, that the shelling would be limited to government headquarters and military targets. But we're learning that people are receiving phone messages from the Israeli military, telling entire families to leave their homes.

My friend Farah calls to tell me that her father has received just such a message, ordering him to evacuate al-Karamah Towers — the neighbourhood in which we, too, live — if he wants to survive. In fact, her father moved out of al-Karamah two years ago. With the little phone credit we have, my friend and I laugh at this situation, and scold the Israelis for not updating their intelligence.

October 10, 2023

Our jokes have become our reality. The things we were able to laugh about yesterday are haunting us now. The Israeli shelling in our area has again intensified; the explosions are dangerously close to our home. A few hours ago, al-Karamah Towers was bombed in a two-and-a-half-hour raid known as a 'fire belt'. My daughter and I called our friends, who live close to the site of the bombing. We told them to come to our house immediately. They said they couldn't come precisely because they were under attack; if they moved, they would be targeted.

I had to tell myself to stay on the phone and keep talking, keep listening, as if I were feeding my soul, saturating myself with their voices for as long as I could, in case I never heard them again.

Tonight, my daughter Habiba and I have decided to sleep in the hallway of the house, believing it to be the safest place. I have run out of reassuring words. Anxiety prevails.

At midnight, we start to hear strange sounds in the neighbourhood. Not explosions, but something else. Carefully, I go to the window and look out to the main street. My fears are confirmed:

all along the street, our neighbours are evacuating. They've received calls from the Israeli Defence Force, warning them to clear the whole area as soon as possible.

Oh God, I'm exhausted and just getting ready for bed. Now, I have to pack our belongings and leave. But where should we go? I have no idea. I don't know anywhere in the universe safer than my own home! Just a few minutes ago, I was telling everyone that I couldn't sleep anywhere but in my own bed. Now, I have to say goodbye to it.

If only I had a suitcase large enough to contain all the walls of my house...but there is no time to think. Only time to fear. We have five minutes. Any longer and my family will be exposed to real danger, perhaps even death. We leave the house trembling with fear and adrenaline.

There are thirteen of us fleeing the area: myself and Habiba; my mother and father; my siblings Mohammed, Nizar and Nagham; and Nizar and Nagham's families. We leave by car, protected by the Red Cross. Shells fall behind us on the streets we've abandoned.

October 11, 2023

Last night, we evacuated to my brother Munther's house in al-Nasr neighbourhood, in the centre of Gaza City. It's less than half a mile from my home, but a much safer place to be, according to the occupation's evacuation orders.

Munther, a doctor, lives in our old family house: the house in which we grew up. Here, we were joined by many members of my extended family: 26 people in total, and not a lot of room to share. But room didn't matter; only safety did.

My daughter Habiba told me about her great fondness for her own bedroom and her attachment to all her belongings. When she realised I'd only brought one pair of her pyjamas and one toothbrush, she became upset.

'It's just for one night,' I reassured her.

Today, around 8am, we left my brother's house and returned to our own. The joy of returning was indescribable. The place felt different, as though it had been rearranged. My room looked beautiful.

By phone, I spoke to students from a creative writing course I have been teaching at the Abdul Mohsen Qattan Cultural Centre—a course disrupted by the war. The students were worried about me, given how close my house is to the occupation's evacuation warnings.

At 3:30pm most of al-Karamah's residents were contacted again by the Israeli Army. This time, we were given an official and complete evacuation notice. I packed a few things—phone, laptop, wallet, clothes and cat—and left again.

Now, we find ourselves and all of our relatives back in our old family house in al-Nasr for the second night running. Our conversation has one subject: how long will this last? Many political analyses are offered. Some predict the war will last only a few weeks; others predict it will go on for many months.

Hearing these conversations in my childhood home—with everyone's worried gaze fixed on the news, and the room heavy with a sense of anticipation—reminds me of the first Gulf War, when Saddam sent 'Scud' missiles over Gaza towards Israel. I was my daughter's age then. Are we destined to keep reliving history over and over?

My sister Nidaa and her family have arrived. My daughter Habiba and her cousin Tamara play with their cats while us adults pass the time with word games and rounds of rock, paper, scissors.

Tomorrow we will pack our belongings and return home.

October 12, 2023

Thank God we are still alive. Thank God for the blessing of a new day.

This morning, I was so excited about the prospect of returning home to al-Karamah Towers that I called two of my sisters, living abroad in America and the UAE, to reassure them about our situation. One was so happy that she cried. I scolded her for being dramatic.

The next minute, I heard screams from inside the house, from the area where my sister Nidaa has made a temporary home for herself. Her apartment had been bombed! The building in which she lives, Presidential Guard's Towers, has been completely destroyed! This was the home she and her husband built together; they sweated and paid for every inch of it. Now, it's just rubble with no value. Now, Nidaa, her husband and her husband's family must live here, in a corner of our childhood home: a space no bigger than 50 square metres.

No words of condolence will help. We will never know why a home has been specifically targeted and destroyed. It's a war filled with secrets. Driven by hate.

Who knows, perhaps my house will be next.

October 13, 2023

THE TOUGHEST DAY

This morning, we woke up to perform the Fajr prayer, only to hear strange movements in the street below. The inhabitants of the tower opposite us had received warning messages from the Israelis; their homes had been selected for bombing.

Our own house was full of children and elderly people, some confined to wheelchairs. Everyone told us we had to move quickly and evacuate to the nearest UNRWA school. But, after an hour, it turned out that the warning to the house across the road was a false alarm. We all laughed at our strange fortune, and headed back to the family house.

Then, at noon, Israeli F-16s started dropping leaflets, urging us to evacuate Gaza City entirely and head to the southern areas of the Strip: to the cities of Khan Younis and Rafah. The Israelis gave everyone a 5pm deadline for evacuation. Anyone who hesitated would be putting their lives in danger.

Yes, it's a forced displacement.

My sister Nidaa, whose house was bombed yesterday, was the first to decide to leave. 'The South will soon be swamped,' she reasoned, 'much better to get there first.'

My sister Nagham, who works as a journalist, chose to follow.

My uncle Akram arranged for a driver to pick him up at 2pm to take him to his in-laws in Khan Younis. But the driver was late, and my uncle waited in his wheelchair on the street for over two hours, surrounded by his whole family: wife, youngest daughter, son and granddaughter. The 5pm deadline came and went. My uncle called the driver and scolded him.

Now, we are hearing that a lorry has been bombed on Salah al-Din Road, and 70 displaced people have been martyred. This is the same road my uncle and his family would be passing along right now, had their driver been on time.

My uncle's evacuation will have to wait till tomorrow. But the bulk of my family — myself and my daughter, my brothers and their families, my parents and my uncles and their families — have all decided to stay.

October 14, 2023

Thank God that we are still alive. Thank God for the blessing of a new day.

Last night was a very difficult night. But eventually we fell asleep, probably out of exhaustion.

My sister left her cat with me: she doesn't have the luxury of keeping a pet while being displaced from one place to another. It turns out that one of the toughest challenges I've faced in the war, so far, is providing food and litter for these two cats. I wonder: should we really be keeping pets in a city like Gaza, when the enemy doesn't respect even the rights of humans? But this is no time for complaining. I have the lives of two more souls on my shoulders, in addition to the lives of my family and relatives.

The era of the queue has begun. Whether in the house or out in the city, queues are everywhere: one queue for bathing, one for water, one for getting bread, one for withdrawing money at the ATM, one for getting essential vegetables from the grocery store, one for charging my mobile. And to think they call us disorganised people who do not like to queue!

It is a beautiful irony that the shops selling pet food stay open until 4pm, while the shops selling human food are closing early.

October 15, 2023

Thank God that we are still alive. Thank God for the blessing of a new day.

It is now the ninth day without electricity or internet. The markets are closed, except for some small shops that do not provide essential supplies. There is a crisis in obtaining women's products. My hair is falling out, my skin is drying up and my weight is dropping. I don't want to be weakened by these deprivations. Weakness cannot be an option right now.

My friends Israa, Farah and I agree we should take turns in communicating. Each of us will be appointed a day for messaging or calling around. We each have limited mobile credit, and limited options for adding more.

Israa has been displaced to Nuseirat City with her friends. Farah has fled to Khan Younis with her relatives.

I'm alone in Gaza City.

October 16, 2023

Thank God that we are still alive. Thank God for the blessing of a new day.

The Israeli occupation have issued announcements and proclamations stating that the Hamas movement is a terrorist entity, and whoever stays in Gaza City will be considered a participant or an accomplice. We receive these announcements via text messages, automated phone calls and leaflets dropped from the sky.

The psychological pressure is increasing. Those who left for the South are already telling us, through texts and phone calls, that they are regretting it. But they cannot return due to the danger of airstrikes on the roads.

Houses everywhere are forced to shelter up to 30 people at a time, with one room allocated for men, another for women and another for children. Even planning to collect water or bread requires complex strategising. Allocations are made one-per-person, but not everyone can stand in the heat all day, queuing. One of the men might be assigned to collect his immediate family's allocated amount of water or bread from a shop, and will then queue again, wearing a hat and glasses, for members of his extended family.

People have resorted to burning wood for cooking and to heat water for washing. Men light the fires; women cook. Vegetable oil is now being used to fuel cars, which are still essential to many for picking up supplies. Food is divided equally into two meals a day per person, and each person is assigned only one piece of bread. People can only afford to wash once a week. We wear the same clothes for days on end, we lack the hot water to wash them with.

This is the Palestinian people in a nutshell: they grumble, then relocate, then they adapt.

October 17, 2023

Thank God that we are still alive. Thank God for the blessing of a new day.

Since I've been living with my brothers' wives Malak and Taghreed, and my cousins Souad, Islam and Kholoud, I've started to learn new recipes and improve as a cook. My talents are modest, but I've been surprising my family with things like cookies, soups, omelettes and cheesecake — each made with our limited supplies of rice, flour, bulgur and eggs.

My daughter still misses her room and her belongings.

October 18, 2023

Thank God that we are still alive. Thank God for the blessing of a new day.

The number of martyrs in Gaza has exceeded 5,000. Because we can only use our generator for an hour a day, we miss the news when it is first announced. Instead, my sisters and friends call me from abroad, crying, giving me the latest updates.

I am thankful I don't follow the news as closely as they do. In these circumstances, following the news is a luxury.

October 19, 2023

Thank God that we are still alive. Thank God for the blessing of a new day.

Today, we are celebrating the sixth birthday of my cousin Khalid's son, Nasser. Another of Nasser's cousins, an artist, makes a cake out of plaster with Nasser's name sculpted on it. We buy some sweets and place them in an elegant bag. We sing and dance.

I can't work out if we're trying to instil joy in Nasser's heart, or trying to cleanse the pain from our own.

October 20, 2023

My sister Nagham has returned from Khan Younis due to the scarcity of resources, the shortage of water and the increasing number of displaced people staying with her husband's relatives.

Through her work as a journalist, my sister has an internet package which works for a few minutes, then stops for hours at a time. She tells me that my friend Faten, who lives in Umm al–Fahm,[1] in the other part of the homeland [Historic Palestine], has been trying to check in on me through WhatsApp.

Back on the first day of the war, Faten told me that the phones of Arab citizens in Israel were being monitored. To avoid putting her in danger, I haven't tried to contact her since. Yet, now, she risks her own safety to check in on me.

Thanks to my sister's internet access, Faten is able to call me. We talk in code to protect ourselves. We cry together in a miserable attempt to console one another, it's the only language the enemy cannot encrypt or block.

After the call, I promise myself that I will block my friend once internet access returns, to prevent her from checking on me and exposing herself to danger again.

October 24, 2023

Thank God that we are still alive. Thank God for the blessing of a new day.

The bombing has reached the churches. Even Gaza's most famous church, The Church of Saint Porphyrius, has been attacked, despite it being well known that the church houses dozens of our Christian brothers and sisters, already displaced from their homes by this war.[2]

The bombing across Gaza intensified as last night drew on. The occupation launched attack after attack on citizens' homes, all of them without warning. We weren't able to sleep until just before dawn.

I'm woken at 6am by a call from my older sister Nihaya, who lives in the United States. It's afternoon there, and she is hysterical. One thing I should explain: putting your mobile phone on airplane mode during the war is absolutely out of the question. This is lesson 101, I now realise.

My sister is desperate to know if we're OK, as a house belonging to the wider Mohana family in the Sheikh Radwan neighbourhood has been bombed, according to reports. She doesn't miss a moment of news, day or night.

I tell her that she's in such a panic, she's forgotten there are no longer any of our family members in the area she's talking about. They have all been evacuated. I remind her that I'd told her this a few days ago.

She responds with more questions: 'How are you... are the family really OK... are you lying just to reassure me?'

I snap back in an attempt to relieve the tension: 'Would the signal be this clear, Sis, if I were stuck under the rubble?'

October 25, 2023

Thank God that we are still alive. Thank God for the blessing of a new day.

Our IQs have been improving, thanks to the intelligence games my daughter Habiba and I play on our mobile phones every day. Miraculously, I've discovered a solution to our fights over the phone charger: when she's charging her phone from the generator, I can charge mine from my laptop — one of the few things I managed to rescue from my home when we fled. Now, my laptop's main job is to act as a power bank.

I'm always relieved when Habiba and I avoid a fight. Last night, before we fell asleep, she even told me she respects me. Though we sometimes fight, she loves how strong I am as a mother.

October 27, 2023

Thank God that we are still alive. Thank God for the blessing of a new day.

On Wednesday, the family of the Al Jazeera correspondent Wael al-Dahdouh was assassinated in full view of the world. Today, we watch the clip of him bidding farewell to his wife, children and grandchild (three generations of his family), with visible shock on his face.

In the evening, it's announced on the news that Israel will cut off all remaining communications in Gaza City. Internet lines will be severed completely in preparation for a ground invasion. We will lose the ability to check on relatives abroad and access urgent news.

The shelling comes closer and closer. The loudest strike is the bombardment of a building just 60 metres away, targeted by two rockets. Our house fills with dust, dirt and fog. Ambulances rush to evacuate the wounded, or perhaps the dead, from our neighbours' homes. We hear loud cries of 'Allahu Akbar.'

Tonight is a difficult night.

We barely sleep for more than an hour.

We wake up not believing that we are still alive.

October 29, 2023

I will thank God tomorrow if we are still alive. I will thank God, who is the only one to thank for any good, for the blessing of a new day.

November 17, 2023

LEAVING AL-NASR

On the first day of November, I stopped writing my diary of this despicable war — not because I was bored and desperate for it to end, nor because I was unable to preserve my memories amid all the trauma. I had simply been writing my diaries in my phone's Notepad app when — much like patience, hope and all our dreams for the future — my phone went the way of so many things in this war and died.

My immediate family continues to bear the consequences of our decision to stay in the North, but we often take pride in our choice, especially when we hear about the difficult conditions of those in Rafah and elsewhere. Still, staying in Gaza City means experiencing a land invasion, not to mention changing your place of residence three, maybe four, times in the space of a month. It means clearing three or four different houses of rubble and preparing them for your family to move into, taping their windows back together and adapting to a new space. It means paying fifteen shekels for a single can of beans. It means seeing corpses lying in the street; it means seeing dogs, cats and other animals growing fat on them.

On November 3, the Israeli Army made the final call for Gazans to leave their homes and head south. Many of our remaining neighbours packed up and walked towards Wadi Gaza, following a route the Israeli forces bomb every day, having been given strict instructions on how much luggage to take with them. The great exodus to the South continued for another four days, not only down Salah al-Din Road, but by additional, more circuitous routes: the beach road and others.

The house we are staying in was suddenly filled with all our neighbours' belongings. All of the precious things they couldn't take with them, they left for us to look after. This, as it turned out, was a blessing rather than a burden; we needed all of it once the Israeli blockade began. Luckily, me and Habiba are the same sizes as my neighbour, Shaima, and her middle daughter Kenzi. So, when we didn't have electricity or water to wash our own clothes, we began borrowing theirs.

Soon, everyone in the neighbourhood had fled except for us and one other family. Al-Nasr Street, once a bustling thoroughfare thronging with people till the early hours of the morning, was now a ghost town. Each day brought more danger and fear. I hadn't realised how much the proximity of neighbours makes the prospect of dying more bearable; dying with friends around would be a mercy compared to dying on our own, with no one to witness our martyrdom or even know we were gone.

The indiscriminate bombing of shops has begun. On November 9, Israeli forces destroyed a cosmetics warehouse belonging to my middle brother, Nizar. Nizar's warehouse contained two floors of merchandise (perfumes, hair and skincare products, etc.), plus a showroom. It also had its own generator, full of fuel, which exploded under the bombardment and caused the warehouse to burn for several hours.

Nizar had intended to accommodate us in the warehouse in the coming days. He'd imagined its sturdy basement would protect us from Israeli bombs. Watching the thick black smoke rising and darkening the sky, I didn't know whether to be grateful for being given another lease of life, or to mourn the annihilation of a life's work, destroyed in front of my brother's eyes.

The following day, November 10, the Israeli tanks on al-Nasr Street were simply too close to our family home, and we decided to move for the second time. We no longer had the luxury of succumbing to depression, or wallowing in the misery of what had already happened to us. We could only think quickly about how to survive the next moment.

As a family, we continued to refuse to be displaced to the South. Instead, we relocated about 300 metres down the road to my cousin Mahmoud's house in the middle of al-Rimal neighbourhood.

That night, we learned that an Israeli tank had parked in front of the home we had just fled. The only other remaining family in al-Nasr neighbourhood had to be evacuated through the back door by the Red Cross, holding their breath the whole time as they ran. In such moments, a simple cough or sneeze, even the accidental passing of wind, can cost you your life. If you have a crying child with you, you're as good as dead. Such is the reality of war.

For the second time, a new life has been written for us.

We are now about 30 people, living in an otherwise-empty tower block: women and children sleeping in a residential apartment; men and teenage boys sleeping in the lobby. The building has solar power: for a few days we were even able to charge our phones, watch our favourite movies and follow the news on Al Jazeera hourly. What a joy! But this respite has been short-lived.

Today, tanks punched through and entered the street.

November 20, 2023

TANK SALUTES

I have known the word 'tank' all my life, but I'd only ever seen them on TV or in epic movies about the World Wars. Today, I saw one through my window. It was approaching, and the closer it got, the more gigantic it became, its wicked cannon swivelling left and right, ready to fire at any time.

I screamed for the others to come, and when they arrived and pulled back the curtains, the tank chose to launch three shells directly at us. The first shell impacted somewhere just below us; it didn't seem to explode. The second shell exploded as we darted back from the window, sending pieces of broken glass flying across the room. The third shell exploded further down the street, just as we reached our hiding places in the inner room. I think, if it hadn't been for the luck of the first shell not exploding, none of us would be alive right now.

As it is, many of us are injured. We've all suffered temporary deafness and Aunt Latifa has a cut across her forehead. But it seems I've borne the brunt of the injuries. Two of my teeth are broken, my upper lip has burst and there's a deep cut on the side of my nose. Everyone is screaming, thinking, from the sight of my blood-soaked clothes, that I am done for.

But I have been granted a new life, it seems, for the third time now.

December 5, 2023

A TEMPORARY TRUCE

After firing its three, random shells, the tank trundled down our street and turned onto another. We went downstairs and huddled together in the guest suite of the building, staying there until we were saved by the declaration of a temporary truce two days later. The tanks did not withdraw. But the moment the truce started, we left al-Rimal and returned, once again, to our old family home in al-Nasr.

Our home here comprises two buildings, with a wide courtyard between them. Each building holds four apartments, and the whole home is usually inhabited by six branches of our family. But almost everyone has left now. A few have even been lucky enough to travel abroad, with the help of children residing in Europe. Most have been displaced to the homes of relatives and in-laws in the South.

The temporary truce only lasted a week. We spent most of that time cleaning up our two buildings, sweeping up broken masonry and shattered glass. We covered the empty windows with nylon; winter is almost upon us.

During the truce, we were even lucky enough to sneak north, to check on our my house in al-Karamah, navigating there in Nizar's car; forced to travel through winding backstreets and alleys because a tank remained stationed at the main entrance to our neighbourhood. As the nearby market in al-Rimal has been completely bombed, we scoured the stalls on the way north for whatever food we could find — this included Sahaba Market, Balad Market and the so-called 'Thieves Market' (where little attempt is made to hide the fact that the produce has been stolen from bombed and abandoned shops).

When I finally stood in front of my house in al-Karamah, a strange reverence overwhelmed me. Tears gathered in my eyes and I prostrated myself on the pavement, chanting words of supplication and gratitude to God, realising His glory only now. I loaded what belongings I could fit into the car, then sat silently in my room, gazing at its walls for over a quarter of an hour. Finally, I gathered up my last load: my old mobile phone and some nail clippers. I haven't eaten eggs since October 7. My nails have started to break.

Another story from the truce...

My brother, Munther, was walking down the street in al-Nasr neighbourhood when a young man appeared from inside a house, surprised to see another soul in Gaza City.

'Who are you?' this young man asked. 'Where have you come from? Why are you outside?'

My brother told him about the agreed truce and explained that people were moving in the streets more normally now.

The young man was shocked, admitting that his family hadn't heard any news for two weeks and knew nothing about any truce. He explained that none of them had dared to go outside after their father left the house and never made it back.

My brother, being a doctor who has treated many of the wounded at al-Shifa Medical Complex, asked for a description of the young man's father, hoping he might remember him.

The young man described his father in detail, and added that he was wearing a brown tracksuit and slippers the day he disappeared.

My brother confessed that he didn't remember anyone matching this description. But about 50 metres down the road, my brother spotted a brown tracksuit lying in the street: the body of the young man's father.

Shortly afterwards, my brother made a similarly horrific discovery: an entire family trapped under the rubble in the remains of their home, each having bled to death while the ambulances were unable to reach them. Among those martyred was a mother with her small dead child still clutched in her arms.

Later, I scoffed at my 'oh so brave' cousin Mustafa, when he told me he had seen pelvic bones, ribs and a whole thoracic cage lying in a pile of rubbish.

I told him that I, too, had seen bodies in the street; that the bones of cats, dogs and horses did not scare me.

'But these bones belonged to people,' my cousin said, 'not animals.'

As soon as the ceasefire ended, on November 30, the danger intensified again. Aerial and artillery bombardment has rained down relentlessly. As a result, we've taken a family decision to stay together in one of our two buildings, hoping this will be safer.

Another tank is stationed at the end of our street: at a roundabout just 100 metres away. Accordingly, a list of prohibitions has been imposed: no lights, no loud talking, no listening to the radio, no leaving the house after 5pm. If we had small children with us, perhaps we would have been bombed on the first night.

I wonder: do the soldiers in the tank watch us as carefully as we watch them?

A few days ago, my uncle became enraged when people accused him of being the loudest snorer. He promptly announced his intention to move back across the courtyard, to our family's other building. The following night, the wall of the room he had been sleeping in was hit by artillery fire from the tank stationed at the roundabout.

When he saw the damage, he was pale-faced and joked, 'Snoring has health benefits.'

WE HAVE BEEN GRANTED A NEW LIFE, FOR THE FOURTH TIME

On December 11, at 7am, the building adjacent to us was bombed. The explosion jolted us into life, but we couldn't see anything through the dust and ash that filled the air. Each of us ran to check on our loved ones. After ten minutes of screaming and panicking, we were reassured that we had all survived without even a scratch. For the fourth time, we had been granted a new lease of life.

Our home wasn't so lucky. Shrapnel had damaged the solar panels and water barrels on our roof, leaving us without power and water, and part of our building was destroyed. Following this, we moved to the basement, taking up residence in the empty apartment of my uncle Nasser, who had left for the South during the truce.

Recently, in Rafah, my sister Nidaa, who's been displaced since the beginning of the war, found herself having a difficult phone conversation with a volunteer delivering food parcels in the North.

Nidaa told the volunteer that we were still living in the old family house, on al-Nasr Street.

But the volunteer swore to her, in all seriousness, that this was impossible. 'It is a street full of ghosts,' he said, 'the whole neighbourhood is completely empty. The tanks have destroyed everything.'

My sister insisted he was wrong, that we hadn't moved.

The volunteer remained unconvinced, and returned with the food parcels undelivered, mistakenly reporting that we had been injured in the recent round of bombing...that we had all been transported to al-Shifa Medical Complex.

Nidaa, the most sensitive of my sisters, fainted upon hearing this. And when she came round, she immediately called our older sister, Nihaya, who lives in America, to pass on the bad news. Nihaya, evidently the second most sensitive of my sisters, also fainted.

For ten days, the rumour of our martyrdom spread further and further afield without us knowing, until today, by pure chance, we discovered a trace of mobile signal on the top floor of our building.

I called my sister Nidaa, who still believed we were dead. Upon hearing my voice, she lost consciousness once again!

December 31, 2023

'I wish I could stretch my back.'

'I wish I could use a proper toilet.'

'I wish I could sleep without the Zanana [the mosquito-like buzzing of the Israeli drones].'

'I wish I could satisfy my hunger.'

These are our wishes on New Year's Eve. Meals are meagre, medicine is nonexistent, even drinkable water has become scarce.

When the tanks finally withdrew, ten days ago, a spate of burglaries spread like a virus across the city. Every morning, we're awakened by the sound of someone calling for help — someone being burgled. My brothers Mohammed, Nizar and Munther and my cousin Mustafa are taking turns patrolling the barely-populated neighbourhood, guarding its houses at night. The Strip has been split in two [by the Israeli-imposed Netzarim Corridor], and the houses of the displaced are the most vulnerable to burglary.

A few days ago, we heard a rumour that my own house in al-Karamah had been set alight by Israeli soldiers, along with most of the houses in the neighbourhood.

January 10, 2024

THE BASATAT MARKET

In Gaza these days, you can't buy anything for less than five shekels — this is what I notice while strolling through the market that spans from al-Shifa Street to University Square. When I saw this market for the first time, I was amazed by the resilience of everyone in it, their determination to rise up and continue striving.

I swear: if the Israeli soldiers could see what I see strolling among these stalls, rather than seeing us through the crosshairs of their tanks and planes, they would convert to Islam in droves.

They would say, 'Bombs: we dropped. Land: we invaded. Displacements: we enforced. Famine: we created. Yet here you still are, displaying your wares: legumes, clothes, air fresheners, sanitary pads, scented tissues, razors, spices, sweets, yeast, knives, spoons... stall after stall, all along the pavement, or what's left of the pavement. Still, the women come and drive bargains with the sellers, as if there were no war! This genocide has cost us a fortune. It's cost us our reputation around the world, forever. Yet here you are, coming to haggle over the price of a winter shirt. Damn you all to hell!'

Except they would say it in Hebrew.

One man in the market is selling cigarettes.

'A single cigarette for six shekels,' he says, 'or two for fifteen.'

I point out that half of fifteen is more than six

He suggests I roll my own.

Grumpily, I tell him, 'I'm no good at rolling my own; I'm merely trying to be straight with you.'

He scoffs. 'There are plenty of buyers and you are just wasting my time, taking up space in front of my stall, arguing. If you don't like it, madam, you can leave. Our prices are fixed.'

January 14, 2024

100 DAYS OF WAR

Today marks 100 days of war; 100 days of being scattered and torn apart; 100 days of loss; 100 days of suffering; 100 days of repeated displacement; 100 days without reliable means of communicating. For 100 days, we've been washing our clothes by hand, cooking our food over firewood, kneading dough as my grandmother did in the 1970s. We have gone back decades. My eldest brother, Nazir, is in Khan Younis, my middle sister, Nidaa, is in Rafah, my youngest sister, Nagham, has left Gaza and travelled to Turkey. But we are still here in Gaza City.

After more than a hundred days of constant bombardment, I want to tell you that we, the people of Gaza, have developed the most extensive vocabulary for describing different types of bomb and other noises of war; words such as:

1. 'Bouf'—aerial bombing.
2. 'Tsoooo'—naval bombing.
3. 'Dddof'—artillery shelling.
4. 'Lululululu'—night illumination flares accompanied by the smell of gas.
5. 'Trak trak trak'—the sound of a quadcopter drone.
6. 'Chik chik chik'—the sound of a tank as it moves.
7. 'Fooof fooof'—the sound of the bulldozer.
8. 'Duf duf tik tik'—the sound of clashes.
9. 'D-duf d-duf'—the sound of a racing heartbeat when scared.
10. 'Duf duf duf duf'—the sound of a fire belt (carpet bombing of a restricted area).
11. '........'—the sound of a rumbling, hungry stomach.
12. 'Wssssss'—the sound of feet running quickly during a bombing, not knowing where to go.
13. 'Waaaaaaaaaaa'—women screaming during a bombing.
14. 'Waah'—men screaming during a bombing.
15. 'Ah'—touching cold water.
16. 'Yuck'—drinking salty water.

Despite our proficiency in distinguishing all these sounds, we have begun to lose our hearing. We have started to ask those calling us from outside to repeat what they are saying over and over, not only because the signal is weak, but due to our own deafness.

They talk, and we repeatedly ask, 'What? What? What?'

We have also set records in:

Collecting the Largest Number of Unexploded Bullets (of All Shapes and Sizes) for Use as Souvenirs.

Consuming Canned Foods, especially baked beans and kidney beans (despite the consequences of eating so many beans!).

Climbing onto Windowsills like a Gazan Spider-Man, trying to get a mobile or internet signal.

Going to Bed Early. There is so little else to do — no internet, no electricity, no TV.

Conserving Mobile Battery. A charge lasts four days because the only thing it's actually used for is games and as a flashlight when going to the toilet at night.

Growing Facial Hair: beards and moustaches, for men; eyebrows and moustaches for women due to the lack of barbers and hairdressers.

Using Nylon and Plastic Sheeting for Windows once all the glass has been blown out.

Using Vegetable Oil for Everything, not just cooking, but in cars in the absence of diesel and gasoline.

Paying Extortionate Amounts for Simple Things. A donkey cart ride, in the absence of any other transportation, is now twenty shekels.

Living with Rubbish. It fills the streets as the municipality hasn't been operating since the truce.

Seeing the Cleanliness of the Sea from a Distance. No one has entered it or contributed to its pollution for four months.

Mosquito Bites.

Cat Sizes. Street cats have been feeding on rubbish and corpses, becoming impossibly fat.

The Longest Dropouts in Internet and Communication Services Since Outages Were Invented.

January 17, 2024

'They keep talking about humanitarian aid that hasn't been allowed to arrive: flour, sugar, rice, milk and medicines. Can we add some other necessities to this list: hope, patience and resilience?'

This is what I post today on Facebook: a post I make merely to reassure my friends that I am still alive. So many have heard the rumours of our martyrdom.

We've discovered an internet signal in the grounds of the American International School, where dozens of families are still taking refuge. Each family occupies a classroom, their name written on its wall. The signal has appeared after a two-and-a-half-month internet outage. The hourly rate to access it is five shekels, and the hours soon add up. But for me, this is the greatest discovery.

January 23, 2024

A LETTER TO MY DAUGHTER

My dearest Habiba,

I apologise for bringing you here.

I apologise for not relocating to a country that respects human dignity. I turned down several offers of fellowships for artists and writers from institutions abroad. I honestly believed we were safe; I did not know that safety had to be bought or planned for. I thought it was a given right.

I apologise for your displaced childhood, for the hours of boredom and for your constant scrolling through your phone, remembering and mourning the beautiful moments of the past.

I apologise for the fact that displaced families have taken shelter in your school, messed up your classroom and played on the swings you used to enjoy with your friends.

I apologise for what you've had to experience: your bedroom burning, your toys scattered, your clothes stolen. You should be somewhere else, spending the best days of your life thinking about your future and hanging out with your friends in amusement parks and shopping centres.

I apologise because you are in the wrong place in the world and it is my fault. My little daughter, they talk about deals and I tell them, to hell with all your trivial deals, the only deal I want now is safety.

On your last birthday, I got you a big map of the Strip, but now I can't find our house on it. Maybe we will redraw it together in another place and time.

I fold this letter and hide it among my belongings, not daring to give it to my daughter.

January 30, 2024

DON'T LOOK BACK

Yesterday, they announced the beginning of negotiations towards a long-term ceasefire. This news left me stuck in front of the TV like a wax statue for hours on end, depleting the charge on the house battery. I was hoping to be the first one to hear the announcement, hoping I could break the news to everyone else, as if I'd get some kind of reward for it. But the announcement never came. What does a drowning person do in our country? He waits and waits, hoping for a miracle to come and change the fact that he's drowning.

Tonight, my daughter Habiba and I scrolled through the pictures on my laptop: family photos of our home, trips, picnics, her first day at nursery, her first day at school, birthdays, summer camps, dabke [folk dancing], camping trips and swimming competitions — images that took us all the way up to her graduation from the sixth grade and the scout group she'd joined before this war.

Touched by nostalgia, sleep overcame us. Little did we know we would soon be awakened to face the hardest night ever, not just since the war started, but since either of us were born. I didn't know that someone could fall so far into the jaws of death and still climb out alive.

At exactly midnight, we heard the sounds of shells and bullets, falling like a downpour. At first we thought that the clashes were some distance away. Everyone knew the tanks had withdrawn a month ago, and the danger had subsided. But these sounds were much closer.

Habiba and I got up from our sofabed and moved into my family's room, separated from ours by only a curtain. This movement, encompassing only a matter of seconds and a couple of metres, likely saved our lives. In an instant, shells and artillery fire started raining through the window and penetrating the walls. Shrapnel flew all around us, puncturing the pillows and the sofabed we'd just been sleeping on.

We were in a state of shock, not knowing what was happening in our own house. Were these clashes between IDF and resistance fighters? Were these Israeli tanks, breaching the barricades and clearing the way to take up new positions? Or were these soldiers, running in the streets with machine guns in their hands? We couldn't tell.

I'd never felt the presence of my own death so close to me. Time blurred out of focus, trapping us in the moment. Our heartbeats raced. Our inhalations and exhalations sped up as we lay flat on the ground, faces down, unable to lift our heads or utter a single word.

The gunfire intensified. The explosions and stun grenades sounded like they were coming from inside the house. The drones hovered low in the street, peering through the holes in our walls and windows — taking photographs, presumably, of the scene inside our house.

The end felt inevitable: *we are dead, everything is over.* A hundred questions ran through my head without a single answer:

Who will tell others we've been shelled or injured?
Will anyone be able to help us?
Where will we be buried and who will mourn the most?
What did we do in this life to deserve such retribution?

Oh world, I am a Palestinian citizen, or a refugee, as you wish, it doesn't matter, but I have never killed anyone and I have never oppressed anyone. I don't even remember lying or stealing. Why all this fear? Why all this terror? Why all this injustice, all this gunfire?

I couldn't bear it any more. I burst into tears, crying helplessly as various items exploded around me: window panes, bits of wall, plant pots and colourful ceramic jars. I felt like my head was imploding. I prayed that I would faint from fear, or slip into some form of unconsciousness, even for a moment, just to take relief from the hell around us. I recited the Shahada, closed my eyes, rested my head on the floor and counted myself among the dead.

I find myself in my daughter's arms.

She whispers in my ear, 'Don't be afraid.'

She asks me to intensify my prayers.

I begin to breathe.

The street outside is silent.

Five pairs of eyes stare at each other, each asking each the same questions:

Have the soldiers moved away?
Is this a dream?
What's happening outside?

I look at my watch. It is 3am.

We endured the madness for three whole hours. If what we've just lived through isn't hell, I don't know what is.

My brother Munther, who lives in the apartment opposite us, gingerly opens the door and peers into the darkness, as if dreading what he might find. He is looking for blood, no doubt, and expecting to find it everywhere.

'Don't worry,' I whisper, 'we're still alive.'

Munther takes a deep breath. He explains that a fleet of 30 Israeli tanks passed through our street under full air and ground cover. He had been hiding with his family in the kitchen the whole time: the furthest room from the street.

Of course, we are residents of al-Nasr Street, living under occupation. The Israeli tanks need no excuse or reason to disrupt our lives. They can pass through our neighbourhood 'as often as the cup clinks against the pot', as the old Arabic expression goes. Unfortunately, our pot exploded into pieces long ago. It's too delicate an idiom to suit the life of a Palestinian today.

As morning breaks, the Israeli Army are dropping leaflets, urging those remaining in al-Nasr and nearby neighbourhoods to evacuate and head to the Deir al-Balah Camp in preparation for a wide-scale campaign of arrests. Entire families are fleeing, packing whatever provisions, blankets and clothing they can carry. But we decide to stay.

February 5, 2024

Today we are celebrating my birthday. I make a cake without eggs — the price of an egg is six shekels — decorate it with cream and light a candle.

I make a wish.

Tonight, like every night, we meticulously check our belongings, count our bags and keep heavier clothes at hand in case the soldiers arrive. We pass the time discussing our plans in case of a raid, fearing the kinds of arrests of men that we've heard about in news broadcasts, cracking jokes to lighten the heavy hours and trying our best to distract ourselves from our lurking fear: that wild animal within us which nobody can tame.

After ten long days and nights, filled with the continuous sound of artillery fire and aerial bombardment, we woke to the sound of people in the street, all of them shouting that the tanks had withdrawn and the place was now safe. We hurried to congratulate each other on being granted yet another new lease of life, perhaps for the fifth time during this war.

Wandering the streets, I took in the destruction left by the tanks and the relentless bombardment of the entire area. Our landmarks have been rendered unrecognisable. Until recently, this was one of the few areas of Gaza City that remained unscathed.

Tonight, as we lie under airstrikes and renewed artillery fire, my daughter Habiba confesses that before the war, whenever I left her at home to study, she would spent much of the time on her phone, browsing TikTok and listening to music.

She asks me to forgive her, then adds that she has also been neglecting her prayers and even skipped fasting for two days last Ramadan without telling me.

I ask her why she's confessing all of this as the bombs are falling.

She tells me that she wants to die feeling brave, without hiding anything from me.

I muster up the courage to tell her that I owe her a confession too. I admit that, before all this started, I used to go to the gym not to exercise, but to meet friends, eat meals with them and smoke shisha in the gym café. This is why I never lost any weight.

But six months into the war, when I weighed myself on a set of scales that we chanced upon in my uncle's apartment, I discovered I had lost twelve kilos — not because of the stupid gym, which I hated, but because of the stupid siege, the scarcity of food and the complete lack of sweets. What we've been able to eat since the beginning of the war, mainly legumes, is barely enough to sustain us. On top of that, I've been doing all the necessary chores: kneading, baking, hand-washing clothes, gathering firewood and walking many miles each day to fetch essentials from the market and the pharmacy.

February 19, 2024

Today, we discovered a new internet network at al-Ghafari Junction, extending down al-Jala'a Street. This is the fifth wi-fi network I've discovered; the previous four have all been disabled by the incursion of tanks. It's like clockwork: every time we discover a random, new network in the street, on a junction, or in a school, the tanks immediately pour into the area and destroy everything, forcing us to start our search again.

This time, though, when I heard that someone had found a network, I honestly wished they hadn't. Truly, being disconnected from the internet during wartime is a blessing. No news is good news.

As if to prove this point, I soon receive a message from the director of an organisation I work for in Ramallah, in the West Bank, which has a branch here in Gaza. Usually, these messages are designed to bolster my mental health, or reassure me about my Gazan colleagues, who have been scattered here and there across the Strip without means of communicating directly. But today, the director speaks very bluntly, informing me that a colleague of ours, Iman, has been martyred.

I ask her to repeat the news, hoping I've heard incorrectly.

She obliges in the same tone, only with more detail: Iman's immediate and extended family have also been killed.

'My God, where does such cruelty come from?' I sigh. 'Why all of this pain? Why all of this loss?'

The director tells me that Iman's extended family were martyred more than two months ago. Following this, Iman's immediate family took refuge in their family house in Khan Younis. But death drew near and claimed them too.

I struggle to comprehend this news. It is the nature of the human mind to not be able to process multiple shocks simultaneously.

February 27, 2024

In the days since Iman's death, I've fallen prey to severe depression, afflicted by the same nightmares night after night. I've confined myself to my room, scrolling through my photos and trawling my memories for hours on end, wondering who might be next. This damn war claims a colleague, a friend, a house, an institution, a street, or a café every day—ripping apart your shared past without a moment's hesitation. I'm avoiding the internet: that devious clown which rains down news of martyred loved ones in between celebrity gossip, horoscopes and trailers for Ramadan soap operas.

Oh God, how does this world accommodate all these contradictions? Are we really children of the same planet?

Today, we started planting seeds in the small space in front of our buildings: potatoes, parsley, okra, rocket and tomatoes. It is, after all, late February. There are barely any vegetables in the market; what's left is priced extortionately.

My grandfather, Nazir, was a farmer. He was driven out of the village of al-Masmiyya al-Kabira in 1948, during the Nakba, and forced to flee to Gaza when my father was only four years old. Sidi Nazir learned a lesson from his displacement: wherever you find yourself, plant seeds. What you plant today, your children will eat tomorrow. It doesn't matter where you are—in al-Masmiyya, in Gaza City, even in Rafah—if you want a harvest, you must not hesitate to plant. Stability is never guaranteed to Palestinians, we must take what we can.

When I was a child, my grandfather had large orchards. We used to visit him every Friday, picking and eating his mangoes, peaches, figs and apples. My grandfather used to provide all kinds of fruit and vegetables to hospitals up and down the Strip. After planting expansive orchards around Beit Lahia, he decided to build a large, two-storey house for his family. He was one of the most environmentally conscious people you could ever meet. He valued clean air above everything.

Four years before he died, at the age of 84, the Israeli Army rolled onto my grandfather's land and demolished everything, every last tree. They destroyed his two-storey house with a single bomb. They claimed it was built on settlement territory.

In just a few hours, the fruits of his entire life's work vanished: the figs, the apples, the mangos, the peaches, the tomatoes and the cucumbers.

Before my grandfather died, he taught all of his grandchildren how to farm. Of course, we grew up and earned our degrees in medicine, engineering and law. But after so many years, the most valuable lesson turns out to be his: plant seeds, plant seeds, plant seeds.

February 28, 2024

It is only late February but it feels like Eid has come early. Flour has finally entered Gaza.

At dawn, we hear people calling in the street, telling everyone to head to the Nabulsi Roundabout on al-Rasheed Street to collect the flour being distributed from lorries there. All this after five consecutive food missions have failed to reach us. Each house is allocated two bags of flour — as white as the moon — and we start preparing the kneading and baking tools immediately. The sense of joy that comes with kneading this pure white flour, not adulterated with the corn flour or barley that has eroded our stomachs and assaulted our taste buds for the last two months, is indescribable.

We prepare pies and tea, and eat as if we've never eaten bread before! News starts to spread that the bakeries will reopen. Does this mean we can bid farewell to the firewood, the fires? Does this mean we can say goodbye to the queues at the baking tents that have popped up everywhere? Is it safe to celebrate yet? Or should we avoid another disappointment and wait?

March 1, 2024

Today, Jordanian planes are airdropping food into Gaza. This is Jordan's response to Israeli restrictions on the entry of aid lorries into Gaza's northern regions.

The planes seem to be dropping the pallets randomly. Some of them land in the sea and float away. At first, men jump into their cars or set out on foot, rushing towards the drop zones. But after a few flyovers, the men give up and simply enjoy the spectacle, waving at the planes like children.

Not a single parachute lands in our neighbourhood; the air drops seem to be focusing on camps to the south, or way up north. I gain nothing from these operations except a headache, not only from the noise of the planes, but from the noise of those cheering and waving.

March 7, 2024

Since the beginning of the war, we Gazans have been playing a beautiful game based on cooperation. This game is called 'From Us, To You'.

I'll give you an example: we provide tea leaves, you provide water. From us: solar panels. From you: a battery. From us: a satellite dish. From you: a TV. From us: a generator. From you: diesel. And so on and so on…

It's rare to find a household which has both parts of any pairing. Indeed, this deprivation is what the occupation wants. But we outfox the occupation through simple community collaboration.

Of course, the system sometimes breaks down. It's difficult to secure the cooperation of certain skilled tradesmen such as plumbers, electricians, or blacksmiths. These tradesmen can start acting spoilt, making demands, requiring transportation to and from a job — and at a time when medics and engineers are working themselves to the bone for hours on end.

The daily rate of any junior tradesman is 200 shekels. Like a private doctor, he takes his fee before examining the patient; before even entering your house to find out what the problem is. Tradesmen have earned a lot of money during this war, enough to guarantee a good future for even their great-grand-children. On top of that, the job brings prestige. Every time a tradesman passes by, everyone in the street waves and craves his approval. Some people even run outside and offer a pack of canned food or a kilo of flour to lure him in.

March 11, 2024

Cooking on a stove or finding a full gas canister are fantasies these days. So, last week, we built an oven from scratch in preparation for Ramadan. We searched for a good spot in the courtyard, sheltered from the wind and sun, and collected pebbles and the finest sand we could find to make bricks. Our neighbour Hossam, a baker, helped us finish the task.

Today, on the first day of Ramadan, my sister Nahed calls from the UAE to assure me the war will end in two months. She asks how we're managing, and how we're acquiring supplies.

I reply, 'Leave it to God.'

Breaking our fast together is a family ritual that's remained constant over the years, in peacetime and in war. Tonight, we watch the Ramadan adverts on TV and find ourselves in tears, thinking about our situation. It seems the Arab world is turning its back on us, and devoting itself to dancing, singing, celebrating and chanting praises. As a Palestinian, you are the victim, you are the forgotten, you are drowning in your worries, you are alone.

No one can save you except yourself.

March 16, 2024

Today, we received a delivery from a friend who has a farm in Beit Lahia: each household in our family has been given two tomatoes, three cucumbers and two green peppers. I can't describe how happy we were as we scoffed down the green salad after four and a half months of not eating anything like it. We've also received a supply of canned food, flour and rice from the nearby mosques.

For the first time in ages, we know what it is to be full. We can stop worrying about what we'll eat at suhoor tomorrow.

March 18, 2024

This morning, we're woken at 2:30am, before the suhoor time, by intensive gunfire and the sound of bombs. It's the second incursion into this area, or is it the third? It doesn't matter. The al-Shifa Medical Complex, just 400 metres from our home, is under siege once again.[3] The people living closest the hospital are being ordered through loudspeakers to evacuate to Deir al-Balah, roughly nine miles south.

The gunfire and clashes extend through the morning and a residential compound, just 40 metres from us, is badly damaged. Written above the entrance to this five-storey compound is the blessing: 'This, by the grace of my God'.

March 20, 2024

Our neighbour Rabi has lost his wife and daughter. He swore they were right beside him as he performed the Dhuhr prayer. When the bombs struck, the young men of the neighbourhood worked furiously to search for his wife and child under the rubble, all to no avail. They had to call one of Rabi's relatives to take him away as he was in shock. Today, they found what remained of his wife and daughter's hair up on a roof. They didn't tell Rabi.

Once again, mobile connections have vanished. We've learned by now: the connection drops just before the tanks close in. Its loss has become an omen. The outage means a ground invasion is planned. Or, the ground invasion happens, and in the process, the signal goes down.

It's the eternal question: chicken or egg? Only the egg costs nine shekels, and nobody remembers what chicken tastes like.

March 28, 2024

We are preparing for iftar [the fast-breaking evening meal] when we hear a cry for help from the direction of a nearby besieged compound. The cry rings out against the complete silence of the neighbourhood. Since the latest siege began, no one has left their house.

At first, we think it's an abandoned child, calling for their parents. But when Munther and my cousin Mustafa go to investigate, they find a wounded woman. The Israeli tanks have been shooting at anything that moves, and both her legs have been shredded by rocket shrapnel. She's crawled about 100 metres from the place where she was hit, finally reaching the main street. We try to call an ambulance a hundred times, but the connection is too weak. When we finally get through to the Red Crescent, they say we're in a 'closed military zone' and no ambulance can reach us. Instead, they ask us to bring her to them. So Munther stops the bleeding, helps her into a wheelchair and takes her to meet the ambulance.

When he returns, Munther tells us that the woman had been trying to find water for her family. Like us, they've been besieged for ten days.

April 1, 2024

Today, on the 22nd day of Ramadan, the Israeli tanks withdrew from al-Shifa Medical Complex. We heard the noise of people in the streets at suhoor time and later learnt, from the news, that there were only 50 Gazans remaining in the hospital, out of the 7000 who had been there when the siege began. This number included displaced people, medical staff and patients. As it withdrew, the Israeli Army ordered the medical staff to go in and retrieve the bodies for burial.

Is the word 'genocide' still controversial to you?

Before iftar, I take a little walk to breathe in the air of freedom. For two weeks of siege, the idea of being out here on the street felt like a dream.

I will not talk about the aftermath of destruction. Nor about the burning of a specialised operating theatre which has treated over a million Gazans. Nor about how many houses were flattened. The thing that catches my attention is that the people in the streets look shorter. I can't work out if it's the effect of starvation, anguish, or just humiliation.

April 2, 2024

Our house in al-Karamah has visited me a lot in my dreams, telling me how lonely it is, and reproaching me for abandoning it — just like the horse who's left alone in Mahmoud Darwish's poem.[4] Repeatedly, I've woken in distress, remembering every last detail, and struggling to go about my day.

After this morning's dream, I feel determined to visit the house. So I set out on foot and walk for a full hour, taking in the destruction of neighbourhood after neighbourhood: al-Nasr, Sheikh Radwan and onwards.

Finally, I arrive at the burnt remains of the home I lived in for seventeen years. I wander around, touch the walls, run in the garden and cast one long farewell look at this place I've loved so much. Then I leave without taking a single picture; without looking back, just like Hanzala.[5]

April 7, 2024

Today is April 7. The war has been ongoing for six months.

We are two days from the end of Ramadan and, as a family, we've agreed to observe the same Eid rituals we observe every year. Each household in our family will take its own group photo and share it in the wider family Facebook group. No matter how many tears are shed in the process, what matters is that we are all alive, even if great distances still separate us.

I go to the internet café round the corner to check on our neighbours after the last invasion. A nice friendship has grown up between me and the other visitors. We've come to miss each other greatly if one of us is absent for more than a few days. After each tank withdrawal, the first thing we do is congratulate each other for having survived, then work out who isn't there and fear the worst, or speculate about them fleeing to the South with no intention of returning.

Here you can bump into anyone: a friend who's been displaced from a completely different part of Gaza, a survivor of a bombing, a former neighbour, or a professor from your university. The funniest thing that happens in the café is when someone starts talking to their overseas relatives through video calls. Everyone in the room, which is no more than twenty square metres, can hear every last detail of every conversation: usually a matter of money transfers and their accompanying conversion fees.

On one occasion, before the latest incursion, a lady, who had been passing by chance, decided to sit down beside me and start asking questions:

'Sister, how's the internet connection?'

'It's fine.'

'How much do they charge an hour here?'

'Five shekels.'

'Sister, do you know anyone who could cash this transfer for me at a low commission rate?'

She said the last sentence with a wink of her left eye, as if she was under international surveillance and was trying to communicate a secret.

I winked back with my left eye, drew close and got ready to whisper.

She looked furtively right and left and nodded twice, urging me to speak.

'No,' I told her suddenly, 'I don't know anyone.'

April 15, 2024

I have always been fascinated by the phrase that flashes up in movies: *Six months later.*

Usually, in films at least, six months is enough time for great things to happen. But in our case, what could possibly follow this:

Victory?

Liberation?

Independence?

Adaptation?

Persistence?

Or maybe just survival, with us thanking God for not having been killed, and for sparing us the evil of fighting.

My friend Wiam told me, over the phone, that she has been craving maftoul [couscous]. She was displaced from her home during the siege of al-Shifa, and returned to find her home empty. It had been completely burgled.

And yet, despite this disaster, her house had survived: it hadn't been bombed, burnt, or bulldozed. Because of this, she was overjoyed and wanted to celebrate with all our neighbours, whose houses, of course, had also been burgled. She wanted to invite them to lunch, and the lunch just had to be maftoul.

So Wiam asked her poor husband to go and buy some cooking equipment, and her poor husband came back from the markets with a used maftoolieh [steamer], which he'd bought from an unfamiliar vendor. This salesman had sworn the maftoolieh was one of the best he'd ever seen; something Wiam's husband was unlikely to find anywhere else. So Wiam's husband, who had already trawled through markets for two hours to no avail, bought the maftoolieh for 50 shekels, and not a shekel less.

My friend Wiam screamed with delight when she saw what her husband held in his hand: 'That's *our* Maftoulieh! Where did you find it?'

Back in the days when my friends and I used to sit and chat, we'd always ask each other one particular hypothetical question: *If you were asked to leave your house immediately, and you could only bring one thing with you, what would you bring?*

One of us would say the Quran, another would say prayer clothes. It was the usual list:

Mobile.

First aid kit.

Laptop.

Passport.

Recipe book.

My perfume and shoes.

My kids' certificates and documents.

My marriage certificate.

Etc.

In reality, however, bitter experience has shown us the true answer. A hundred per cent of the time, it is actually: nothing.

By the way, my grandfather's house here in al-Nasr, the old family house in which we were born and raised, is the only building in the area that seems to have held on through this war. Like a tree, many houses have branched off and been destroyed: my father's house, the houses of my uncles Nasser and Abdul, the houses of my Uncle Ismail's children. But the original tree still stands.

It's ironic. Before the genocide, this house which shelters us now was going to be sold to an investor to be pulled down and replaced with a shopping mall.

NO MEN ALLOWED

When my house in al-Karamah, in the far north of Gaza City, was burnt, the fire engulfed everything: clothes, belongings, furniture, beds, shoes, perfume bottles, cosmetics, my brightly coloured scarves, my papers and work contracts, drafts of my novels, training certificates, and my daughter Habiba's toys, books, stories, school bag and summer and winter clothes.

Also burnt were a hundred copies of my latest novel *No Men Allowed:* copies I had had shipped to Gaza from Beirut, with great difficulty. They'd arrived in three stages during the COVID-19 lockdown, two years ago. I kept them in my room, sealed in a special closet.

After the fire, not a single copy remained — not a sentence, not a word, not even a letter.

I've often imagined the soldiers in my house before they set fire to it all, snatching the copies...turning them over...laughing mockingly, then throwing them away and ordering the burning. Who gave them the right to tamper with my history? What danger did the copies of my book pose to them?

Repeatedly, an irresistible thought has crossed my mind. Before the war, I'd sent ten copies of *No Men Allowed* to a local bookseller named Ayman. How lucky I would be if some of these copies remained with him and hadn't been sold. I'd even tried to contact him, but his phone number, WhatsApp and Instagram account all failed to answer. My hope of obtaining the elusive copies began to fade, and I started to come to terms with the idea of loss.

Today, I've been walking for a full hour in pursuit of karak [spiced tea] when, out of nowhere, Ayman the bookseller steps in front of me, smiles and says: '*No Men Allowed.*'

I'm surprised he remembers, despite all the destruction and the way the occupation strives to erase our memory, along with everything else in the city. I hesitate to ask him about the unsold copies. It suddenly feels inappropriate. Too much has changed and, like all of us, he has lost a lot of weight, to the point where I barely recognise him. Besides, his bookshop, beloved for its amazing decorations built from spirals of books, has disappeared, along with its luxurious padded chairs and its countless heaving shelves — now replaced by a small stall and a simple rug.

But the sheer coincidence of us bumping into each other in such a strange place overwhelms me, and before I can muster the courage to shyly ask my question, he declares that he has five copies of my book left. Five! Has a writer ever been so happy to hear their books haven't sold?

I return home, cradling the copies like babies under my arms, the search for karak tea completely abandoned.

April 22, 2024

THAI SHAWARMA

Shawarma is available in Gaza City again, specifically at the famous Thailandy Restaurant,[6] which is one of my favourites. I can barely believe in the existence of the shawarma till it's firmly in my hands. Because of its high price, I am satisfied with just one order. I share it with Habiba, a shawarma lover like me.

I have convinced Renad, my manager in Ramallah, that I will lose my mind if I remain without work. Before the war, my work involved training children in creative writing skills, supporting them psychologically to overcome their crises and challenges and helping them express their experiences through stories.

With surprise in her voice, Renad asks if I'm sure I have the ability to work.

I tell her that I'm more capable than ever before. Letting me work is almost the only way to save me in this situation.

She asks me if I am ready to start as soon as possible.

I want to answer by pointing to my chest: *Yes, this heart is still strong and can listen and absorb the stories of all the amazing children of the North.* But she won't see this grand gesture; today's weak internet prohibits a video call.

I simply answer: 'Yes, I am ready.'

May 6, 2024

THE INVASION OF RAFAH

Leaflets have been dropped on the residents of Rafah in the South, supposedly a safe zone, urging them to evacuate. As everyone expected, and as the Israeli government threatened, the ground invasion of Rafah has begun.

The people of Rafah are fleeing to the supposed safe areas of al–Mawasi, Khan Younis and the Deir al–Balah Camp, leaving their homes to the whims of tanks and thieves. The invasion is expected to continue for months.

May 9, 2024

THE OCCUPATION OF THE RAFAH CROSSING

The Israeli Army have taken full control of the Rafah Crossing [since the start of the genocide, the crossing had been the only way for Gazans to leave the Strip, and only with Israeli permission]. Students, the wounded and the sick will no longer be able to leave. Gaza will become a vast graveyard, at the mercy of an insatiable enemy. The entry of medicines, treatments, aid and food will stop. Shawarma, meat, chicken and eggs will disappear. We will return to canned tuna, white beans, halva and fava beans, in preparation for another famine in the North.

May 11, 2024

THE INVASION OF JABALIA

I'm standing in front of the house in al-Nasr Street, trying to get an internet signal when, all of a sudden, crowds of people start flocking into the neighbourhood, heading towards the schools, bringing cars and donkey carts loaded with mattresses, blankets, luggage, cooking pots and bags of flour.

I'm dumbstruck at first, till a woman shakes me and asks, 'Sister, do you know anyone here who sells brooms?'

I raise my finger and gesture towards a nearby shop which sells household appliances. By this point, the street is full, and the privacy I was seeking has completely disappeared.

Suddenly, the lady returns, groaning and announcing that the seller was demanding twenty shekels for the broom.

'Without a stick!' she adds, throwing her hands in the air, 'For what? Is it God's Holy Broom?'

I ask, 'Why do you need a broom so urgently?'

She informs me that the occupation has entered Jabalia.

In the blink of an eye, the nearby UNRWA schools and al-Suwaidi clinic are filled with displaced people.

May 15, 2024

On the first morning after the arrival of the displaced Jabaleeya [people from Jabalia], we woke to the sounds of a family quarrel coming from the direction of one of the schools. On the second morning, we woke to the sounds of a quarrel between neighbours within the school. On the third morning, we woke to the sound of gunfire as a result of a quarrel between neighbours in the school.

Today we did not wake at all, we had become used to it.

The displaced stay up all night in schools, chanting and singing with loudspeakers, or playing card games like Hand Rummy and Tarneeb [a variant of Whist]. Their presence brings a pleasant buzz of noise to the neighbourhood, in the voices of children, or vendors at their stalls talking to customers. But finding internet coverage on the street has become more difficult. The Jabaleeya are lining up and blocking the street day and night, leaving no space to talk or even browse.

Fortunately, we've found a nearby provider who's offered to extend cables to our home, which is the best news ever. We can now browse the internet while sitting in our pyjamas on the sofa, while drinking tea or coffee, without having to get dressed and cover our hair for the outside world.

What joy!

Almost as soon as I go online, my friend Asmaa calls me from Canada. When I pick up, she collapses and can't stop crying.

Through her tears, Asmaa asks me hundreds of questions, all at once. This is the first time she's heard my voice since October 7. She can't believe I'm alive. She says that her heart jumped out of her chest when she saw a green dot next to my profile picture on Facebook.

I inform her, calmly, that I am indeed alive, and that my daughter and I have been displaced several times, and that my house has been set on fire, and that I don't have enough clothes to wear, and that I've returned to my work despite the impossible circumstances, and that we experienced famine during the month of Ramadan, and that we were besieged three times by tanks. And that...and that...and that...

All the while, she cries.

16 May, 2024

The house adjacent to the one whose internet we've been plugged into has been bombed. Wires flew in all directions and the internet was cut off. After one day of luxury, we are back to using street internet and eSIMs [virtual SIM cards, which became useful following the destruction of Gazan telecommunications providers and Israel's ability to block existing SIM cards], wearing our outdoor clothes to make phone calls, braving the eyes and ears of passersby.

May 23, 2024

WORKING IN A TENT

Today, I'm resuming my work with children as part of the education team for the Tamer Institute for Community Education. One of my tasks is to compile a special 'children's dictionary' relating to the war.

UNRWA has allocated us a tent at Salah al-Din Boys School, in which to carry out activities. My real worry is: what can I possibly offer these kids? I have seen them queuing for water, queuing to receive food stamps, waiting in front of the medical examination rooms. Should I really ask them to write stories? How will stories benefit them? Should I ask them to write their own histories while they have no sense of a future? Should I envy them for their innocence? Or should I pity their coming days that have no horizon?

I start my session by asking the children how many times they've been displaced?

First child: 'Twice.'
Second child: 'Five times.'
Third child: 'Ten times.'
Tenth child: 'Twenty-three times.'
Last child: 'Er, I've lost count!'

Between sessions, I walk through the school, now a shelter to so many displaced people. As I walk, I stumble over the rubble that's scattered everywhere and watch the arrival of even more displaced people. I break up fights between boys waiting in the queues and appoint myself umpire for the girls' competition to see who's fastest at carrying containers of water.

Suddenly, something heavy sails past my face, almost taking my head off, and landing with a heavy thump on the ground in front of me. I hear a man shouting at his children from one of the school buildings, 'That's what happens to your food when you don't listen to me!'

I look down. A dented pressure cooker lies at my feet. If my steps had been any faster, my head would've been under it, and instead of dying from shelling, famine, or siege, I would have been a martyr to the angry father and his flying kitchenware.

I walk on, adjusting to the feeling that I, once again, have been given a new lease of life, perhaps for the twentieth or thirtieth time. I've lost count.

June 1, 2024

Yesterday, the Israeli Army withdrew from Jabalia. By sunrise, the displaced people had returned to wherever they had come from, and a sense of loneliness had returned to our neighbourhood.

June 2, 2024

The internet signal seems strong enough to support a whole half hour of voice calls: magical in these circumstances. To my surprise, my manager, Renad, suggests that I go to the beach for an afternoon to help with my stress, assuming it is safe to do so.

'How far is the sea from your house?' she asks.

Practically speaking, it's about 700 metres away. Existentially speaking, it is two destroyed neighbourhoods and four ruined schools away, all along a street filled with rubble, debris, broken glass, burnt children's toys and the remains of furniture. A street that was once among those closest to my heart.

Renad tells me how strong I am. She will not allow me to wear myself out or lose my sense of self, she says. Too many people need me. She also predicts the war will end soon. I can't tell if she truly believes this, or if she is just trying to give me hope, to make the days pass quicker.

June 18, 2024

Today, on the third day of Eid al-Adha, we held a festival with circus shows in the schools where displaced children are staying, both in al-Daraj and Shuja'iyya.

My colleagues and I danced, screamed and sang with the kids, as if we too were children longing for some joy after so many months of worry. After the singing, we wandered through the area's old streets and popular markets, happy to feel the presence and companionship of other people.

Fate and, arguably, bad choices have led me to be a woman without a man for the last thirteen years. This has been a source of constant conflict between me and my family. I wish I had remarried before the war. Life would be so much easier if I had a partner to share my sorrows with.

My devastated country still cannot accept the idea of a woman living without a man, and still actively punishes those who abandon married life, as if their loneliness and exhaustion in facing all this hell isn't punishment enough. That said, this war has taught me there are harsher things than single life. In war, at least, men and women are equal. Survival is for the strongest, regardless of gender.

June 27, 2024

My friend Rania, who currently resides in Egypt, does not believe in gender equality, despite working in women's organisations for years. I excuse her because she has not lived through the farce of war and has not discovered what we've discovered. Women here break firewood, light fires, stand on stalls selling goods, carry water cans and queue in bakery lines. Men here cook food, feed children, prepare bread and clean the ovens. All duties are shared.

Over the phone, Rania tells me she was walking in the streets of Cairo yesterday when she saw a woman showing all of her flesh, not covered up by anyone. She asks me if I have ever seen such a scene in Gaza? I cry to myself because she does not know about the Gazan men lined up in the street and stripped by the Israeli soldiers while they are arrested from their homes at night.

Heaps of cruelty, betrayal, humiliation and violation! This war has dug its claws into everyone's flesh and no one has escaped its ferocity. Men are no longer men. Women are no longer women. Children are no longer children.

July 9, 2024

THE RECORDINGS AND THE WATERMELON SYMBOL

Today, our phones received a recorded message from the Israeli Army, instructing us to evacuate to Deir al-Balah immediately. What a tireless enemy. It seems our area is now designated a 'danger zone' along with al-Rimal and Tel al-Hawa.

The maps on the leaflets they drop from their planes divide our territory into green and red areas, exactly like a watermelon. Since the beginning of the genocide, our cause has been represented online with the watermelon symbol, perhaps to escape social media algorithms which censor our flag. In the process, everyone has adopted the symbol, reposting and res-ignalling their politics, but forgetting the actual cause.

When the occupation's leaflets first fluttered from the skies, they terrified us. Later, they worried us. Now, they cheer every-body up. We can burn them on our fires to heat our dignity-flavoured morning coffee.

July 12, 2024

FREE THERAPIST

We remain under siege. Our work has been suspended, due to the danger of leaving our homes and the occupation's targeting of schools. For the sake of our mental health, the NGO I work for has appointed a psychologist to hold group sessions via Zoom.

Today is our first online meeting. When my turn to speak comes, I speak for an hour and a quarter, ignoring all attempts to silence me. I pour out my heart, unburdening myself of the weight of mountains, scattering sentences and unconnected words, almost delirious. The others in the Zoom room gradually begin to disappear, perhaps in search of Acamol tablets. Eventually I'm alone with the therapist, who looks at me with compassion and sympathy.

I've spilled my heart, but the grief hasn't left me because the siege has not ended. We've become used to this . . . this weight. Astonishment and terror have died in our hearts and indifference reigns supreme. Despite this, the siege has a pungent taste: its night remains heavy, its day is long and mean.

Oh God, how things have changed. Before the war, we used to get annoyed by the sounds coming from the streets: and the yells of children playing football and the voices of street vendors who didn't sell anything worth buying. Now, we miss the voice of the refrigerator seller. The sound of the fresh water carts would be a symphony to our ears.

Our grandparents remembered their fields and we remember our houses. What will our grandchildren remember?

July 23, 2024

IN OUR HOUSE, THERE IS A GAS CYLINDER AND A MOUSE

The genocide has not made me a superwoman and living through war has certainly not changed everything about me as a person. I'm still afraid of mice and still I hate white beans.

A few days ago, I noticed a mouse wandering around the house and was instantly terrified. I used traps, glue and old tools to try and catch it, but I couldn't find cheese. I needn't have worried, the mouse soon despaired of finding anything nourishing to eat and left of its own volition.

25 July, 2024

RED CROSS COUPON

Today, the school I am teaching at was bombed. A piece of shrapnel flew through the air and penetrated our NGO's tent, injuring the Quran teacher, who was surrounded by fourteen teenage boys. The teacher was quickly tended to and removed from the school for treatment.

An hour later, in a different part of the same tent, my students gather around me, trying to finish what we started before the bombing: an exercise in collective writing.

24-year-old Nisreen tells me she isn't used to asking for help, that she is happy to be strong and not expect anything from anyone.

I tell her that, despite her pride, she must be prepared to receive the gifts of heaven, which come in the form of a pat on the back from God. Sometimes strength can deprive us of such gifts.

'But our sky throws shrapnel, not gifts,' Nisreen replies, making us all laugh.

Fifteen-year-old Raghad tells us about the difficulty of hauling gallons of water to the fourth floor of the school every day. She and her sisters have to manage this task alone due to their parents' old age and the absence of their brothers, who are abroad for study and work purposes.

Sondos, also fifteen, concludes the meeting by asking us to join her prayers for a Red Cross coupon.

'Why a Red Cross coupon in particular?' I ask.

She tells us that among the things it grants is...Nutella.

August 22, 2024

BACK TO SCHOOL

When I was told that my next work destination would be the Latin Patriarchate School, I couldn't believe it. How would it feel to pass through the gates of a school I had myself attended in the late eighties and early nineties?

Would I meet my old teachers? Could I still find my way to my classroom? What about the school stage, from which Sister Sirin would recite lectures and hymns? What about the church I entered as a child? A child who hadn't yet formed her personality; a child trying to understand her life and her world, scribbling on walls and blackboards.

The journey to the school takes an hour and a quarter, given the lack of transportation and the debris on the main roads. I take Habiba with me to accompany the little girl I once was. Now I am...what?

A child?

A mother?

A teacher?

The girls in the school have diverse hobbies and passions. Some draw, some compose songs and some come in fretting about waking up early and not being in the mood to learn anything. I train them and Habiba in the art of creative writing. Despite their mood swings, the girls apply lipstick and sip Nescafé from a shared mug with a broken handle.

In this way, they're the complete opposite of us: we have plenty of mugs, but no Nescafé.

Al-Sahaba Market is about 400 metres away from the house, but takes twenty minutes to reach on foot. Before the war, it was not a market, but a residential neighbourhood. Now, it has become a centre of commerce, selling all types of necessities on stalls and boasting the largest trade in stolen coupons. Here, toilet roll is sold for three shekels per section, and a single egg can go for as many as nine shekels.

I usually visit al-Sahaba twice a week, for the purpose of shopping, entertainment and passing the time. But since we ran out of gas cylinders, I have started visiting a lot more often to buy pies, pastries and falafel sandwiches with tahini. As for coffee, it has become a fairy tale here in Gaza; the preparation that took four minutes when gas was available, takes 45 minutes when you're forced to break up wood and struggle to light a fire before you can even think about boiling the water.

I remember the first day I succeeded in lighting a fire by myself and saw the red flames licking the wood. I screamed out loud, crying 'fiiiiyerrrrrrrr,' exactly like Tom Hanks's character in *Cast Away*: a primal scream of man's superiority over nature.

These days, I use a little nail polish remover to help the firewood catch faster. We have a surplus of nail polish remover due to my family's former trade in cosmetics, perfumes and everything that an elegant lady needed back when ladies were elegant.

September 13, 2024

THE PRICE OF AN EGG IN GAZA IS 14 SHEKELS

'Is it a golden egg? Does anyone actually buy them?' This is what I asked the vendor when he mentioned the price of a single egg had jumped again to fourteen shekels.

As a result, eggless cakes and eggless omelettes have become common in Gaza. We've removed eggs from our culinary vocabulary.

So today, when I receive a message informing me that I'm eligible to receive a carton of eggs from an UNRWA voucher, I'm overjoyed. I carefully hide the carton inside a plastic bag, fearing the envy of passersby and the curiosity of vendors. When I arrive home, cheers and kisses erupt as if I have brought al-Aqsa with me![7] We prepare a plate full of eggs fried in olive oil and literally, not metaphorically, nibble our fingers afterwards.

September 15, 2024

THE BARBICAN THEATRE

Yesterday, my diaries were read in English at the Barbican Theatre in London. The Barbican is a British institution which people visit from miles around with a passion for art, not politics.

On Friday, I made sure to message all 25 of my English friends — writers, artists, photographers, theatre professionals and musicians — and urged them to book tickets quickly. Half an hour later, the theatre management informed me that all 280 tickets had sold out within hours of the event being announced. I was able to secure only one VIP ticket, which went to my friend Jehan, who offered to film the reading for me.

My diaries were read alongside those of several other Palestinian writers, who have also been documenting their daily experiences since the first day of the genocide, preserving the Palestinian narrative during wartime. Our words were spoken by celebrities and actors, and I didn't fully comprehend the magnificence of this event until my friend Jehan sent me a video. Laughter erupted and the audience's hearts raced as the actress Maxine Peake read from my January 14 diary entry describing the sounds of war and the unusual records Gazans have set during this genocide.

Hearing my diary read in one of Europe's most famous

theatres while I'm here in Gaza is one of the most beautiful things in this strange world.

6 October, 2024

THE SECOND INVASION OF JABALIA

A full year has passed since the war began.

For the second time, tanks surround Jabalia Camp, besieging hospitals and preventing free movement. Once again, displaced people flock to al-Nasr carrying luggage, water barrels, food and drink boxes, blankets and mattresses. They've learnt the harsh lesson from the first invasion: when you flee, take everything you can carry, but discard whatever memory and hope you can spare. Memory and hope are useless in such times.

October 15, 2024

A week after entering Jabalia, the occupation expanded the evacuation area to include al-Nazla, the end of Sheikh Radwan and the outskirts of al-Jala'a neighbourhood, having already established themselves in Beit Hanoun and Beit Lahia in the far north.

How shameless!

The occupation dares to infiltrate Beit Hanoun during the olive season. Don't they know this is one of the most important seasons for the residents of this area, whose rituals have only just begun? Many residents have abandoned their trees, leaving ladders hanging from the trunks; some have even left their shoes and winter clothes behind, believing the military operation will take only days or weeks.

October 17, 2024

WISDOM TOOTH EXTRACTION AND SINWAR'S ASSASSINATION

This afternoon, I am returning from the dentist's office — the only one still open to receive those in need — feeling dizzy and exhausted. I hold one hand over my cheek. My wisdom tooth has just been extracted.

To ease the pain and prevent complications, my dentist recommended that I find a cold drink. This novel medicine is an alternative to the traditional recommendation of painkillers, which are in short supply due to ongoing road and crossing closures and the occupation's obstruction of medical supplies entering Gaza. Unfortunately, a cold drink is just as elusive as painkillers.

One vendor tells me that a kilo of sugar is now 60 shekels!

I ask for ice cubes instead, I don't need sugar and flavourings to ease the swelling.

The vendor replies that, with no solar panels and no diesel for his motor, he stopped selling frozen goods a few days ago, and has now switched to selling candles, earplugs, sewing spools, silicone heat sticks, matches and rolls of tape.

My dizziness returns, just as I hear the sound of people screaming in the street: 'They've assassinated Sinwar! They've assassinated Sinwar!'[8]

For a moment, I think I'm hallucinating — a side effect of the pain. I take a detour home, still searching for a drink. When my phone connects to the internet, after a solid fifteen minutes of false starts, I find the news pages buzzing with the news.

November 6, 2024

TRUMP AND THE FUTURE OF GAZA

Today, Donald Trump won the US presidential election. In a few months' time, he will be officially inaugurated into the White House. What will be the repercussions of this event for the Palestinian cause in general, and for the war of extermination in particular?

I hear a driver saying to his passenger, 'I swear to God, he won't let us go!'

But the passenger is optimistic and seems to be a keen reader of the inner workings of politics.

I tell them both that Trump's inauguration will be good for us in the short term; but in the long term, it will truly lead to the complete 'dissolution' of the Palestinian people.

November 20, 2024

NESCAFÉ IN GAZA

Since the outbreak of war, we have been suffering from a shortage of coffee. When we do find it, it's very expensive, reaching 90 shekels per ounce. Worse, I soon discovered that the coffee we have is adulterated: mixed with chickpea flour. I'd be in the middle of writing reports or talking to my neighbours, and I'd suddenly fall asleep.

Then, in August, Nescafé returned to the northern markets. Its price was 400 shekels, and no one had enough to buy it. For several days in a row, I passed the vendor and examined one of the jars, curious to know how many crazy people we have here willing to buy coffee at that price.

Suddenly, a thought occurred to me: *What if I'm the one who's crazy enough to buy it?*

This was followed by an even more beautiful thought: *What if I share the exorbitant price with others who care about their mental health.*

Indeed, a search was launched for crazy people, and I soon found enough of us to purchase a jar. I put up half the money and, after purchasing the jar, divided the coffee in measures of standard 'teaspoons' (to ensure fairness and quell fears of fraud), in proportion to each person's contribution.

When I returned to our house, I found a gift from my sister and brother in Southern Gaza, sent specially through the checkpoints with the help of a foreign aid worker: two jars of Nescafé, purchased for a quarter of the price I had paid. Fearing that the half-empty jar hidden in my clothes would break, I fought back a faint, not from joy, but from sadness over the 200 shekels I had wasted.

November 22, 2024

A WEDDING AT THE SCHOOL

When one of my students invited me to her cousin's wedding, I assumed it would be held at their home. But when she told me that the wedding would be held at the Amir al-Mansi School, that the platform used for morning assemblies would be used as a makeshift *loge* [a raised platform for the bride and groom] and that one of the classrooms would be designated as a bridal suite, I decided to attend.

Here, I thought, *is one of those things that will happen only once in a lifetime.*

Today, the bride wears a white dress, veil and wreath. The groom wears a black suit and tie. The bride and groom's sisters have been to a beauty salon. They wear makeup and evening gowns.

At the service, the groom is escorted through all the class-rooms, across three floors of the school. I hear they've even managed to hold a traditional 'groom's bathing' ceremony, using the public bathroom.

The guests are treated to lokma [deep-fried dough balls], Aleppo fingers, Arabic coffee and iced water. Every displaced family has cooperated to make this wedding happen, despite the difficulty. Our customs and traditions cannot be abandoned, even if war seems to render them impossible.

November 25, 2024

FAMINE IS KNOCKING ON
GAZA'S DOORS EVERY TWO HOURS

'Breakfast is late, lunch is at 6pm and dinner is cut short.' This is the motto of the people of the Northern Gaza Strip.

Famine has returned due to skyrocketing prices, merchants' monopolisation of food supplies, and the interruption of gas supplies due to Israel's continued closure of the crossings.

What mitigates the impact of the crisis on Gaza's residents is the continued provision of food parcels from humanitarian organisations. These parcels contain canned beans, peas, fava beans, raw chickpeas, lentils and pasta. Some merchants, however, purchase these parcels from beneficiaries and sell them at double the price.

And why might beneficiaries sell their food parcels? In order to obtain cash.

Since the first weeks of the war, ATM machines have been out of action, and cash can only be acquired through the merchants, who pocket 30 per cent commission. So the price of acquiring cash is approximately a quarter of your salary.

Despite this, the current situation is much better than the beginning of the war. Since the bakeries have been operating, we have been able to buy baked goods, lokma flatbreads, luncheon meat pies and falafel sandwiches. Vendors use large quantities of wood for cooking, while bakeries rely on diesel to operate their machines.

Fishermen go to sea to catch crab, which sells for exorbitant prices and is served in soup dishes. Sea bream and salmon are also for sale, a relief for all those stomachs tired of canned food, especially tuna.

As for vegetables: they provocatively sprawl on the stalls like prostitutes, winking and whispering, 'Try me. Our prices are rising daily. If you're brave, come closer and ask about the cost of aubergines, potatoes, cucumbers, or molokhia.' These are the vegetables currently available; we've begun to forget the taste of the rest. Garlic, for example, is sold here by the clove, not the bulb.

December 8, 2024

This week, we implemented a 'tent-to-tent' campaign in the Sohbet Khair Camp. The camp accommodates a large number of displaced persons from Beit Lahia, Beit Hanoun and Jabalia.

Children and mothers gathered around us, eager to write, colour, draw and partake in arts and crafts. Aid organisations distributed health and food parcels, clothing and mattresses, while my team distributed bags filled with pens, paper and crayons. We moved from tent to tent drawing twinkling stars, smiling faces,and playing with the children of the North. All week long, the children's joy was too much for our cameras. Whenever we captured a beautiful shot, we replaced it with another even more beautiful photograph seconds later.

To hell with the occupation.

December 22, 2024

FRUIT SALAD IN GAZA

Today, on December 22, something very important happened in Gaza, surpassing Trump's statements, the ceasefire negotiations, the assassination of Hassan Nasrallah,[9] the fall of the Assad regime in Syria and Israel's skirmishes with Iran.

Fruit has entered the North...and not only through the markets, but also through food parcels: a contribution from the relief organisations whose love has touched us during this war.

Today, I set about cutting the bananas into circles, apples into squares and persimmons into triangles. I drink a glass of fresh orange juice. Two glasses! Our people have been suffering for months from winter illnesses, the flu, coughs and colds due to weak immunity. But now, in front of me, I have a large plate of happiness and vitamin C.

December 25, 2024

The school I'm working at in Sheikh Radwan was bombed twice today: once before I arrived and once after I left. For a moment, I wonder if I'm being targeted. It's a strange coincidence, but my good luck is even stranger!

January 1, 2025

The rain has been heavy. Heavy on the tents. Heavy on the fatigue, the pain and the waiting. Those living in the tents have suffered most, cursing the world and its people. A week ago, they were fleeing the occupation; now, they are fleeing the rain.

Yesterday, my daughter was taking her midterm exam online when her connection cut out at the last minute. She lost the test and her chance to pass, all because of the rain and the winds. I tried calling her teacher, her principal and the entire school board to salvage the situation, but no one answered. It was New Year's Eve and everyone was getting ready to celebrate. It was the heaviest day of the year, and I was begging for any response to my calls. My daughter collapsed in tears beside me.

January 5, 2025

YOU DON'T REMEMBER EVERYTHING

One of the most complex aspects of war, the hardest to understand, is its effect on relationships. A friend with whom you have a long history is now more distant than your temporary neighbour, who receives a coupon and stands behind you in the bread line.

154

How will I console my close friend, who lives in Canada, when she tells me about her depression after someone rear-ended her car? How do I tell her that the struggle of obtaining today's bread, or receiving a feminine hygiene package, has become more important to me than her, her car and our entire friendship?

My temporary neighbour knows all this and more. As soon as we meet, they understand how I spent the night and what my day will be like, because our problems are the same. And as soon as we begin to chat, we find that the problems are over because they are shared. Whoever among us finds a solution to any problem, she tells all her neighbours, and we implement it immediately.

War doesn't recognise history; it only recognises geography.

As for my other friend, who lives in Umm al-Fahm [in Historic Palestine]: I have become responsible for her psychological treatment. She has suffered a relapse because of me. Since the first day of the war, she has worried about me. When I'm offline for hours at a time, travelling here and there and unreachable by phone, she thinks a missile has hit me and I'm lying in surgery, having shrapnel removed from my body. She's been admitted to hospital several times in my place due to nervous breakdowns, lack of sleep, headaches, exhaustion. She follows the news minute by minute, wanting to be the first to tell me that they've reached a deal to end the war.

If healing were in my hands, I would have healed myself first, instead of treating her for the trauma I've caused her as a result of the war.

January 15, 2025

THE DECISIVE MOMENT

After days, weeks, months of delay — what felt like a lifetime of delay, but amounted to 466 days, or fifteen months — it is here.

At exactly 8pm today, a ceasefire was agreed upon in the Gaza Strip, thanks to the efforts of mediators from Qatar, the United States and Egypt. We receive this news while anticipating the press conference during which the details of the deal and the agreed-upon terms will be announced. We drink tea, eat kunafa [a sweet made with thin, shredded phyllo dough] and celebrate like never before. It doesn't matter what we celebrate with, just that we celebrate. There has never been such a thing as a 'celebration' before this day. The people of the North rejoice, the people of the South rejoice. Our families will soon be reunited, the tents dismantled, the displaced returned to their homes, even if they are just rubble.

Gatherings of people can be heard after midnight, displaced people are shouting and singing, guns are fired in celebration.

Rania, my friend in Egypt, texts me: 'The only victory in this war is survival.'

She managed to escape last April, before the Rafah Crossing was closed and taken over by the Israeli Army. She adds that she feels ashamed not to be here in Gaza, at this moment, to celebrate with the rest of her family and friends.

I tell her that our joy today is unmatched in the universe. In disbelief, we check that our limbs are still in place, that our souls have survived.

January 16, 2025

My daughter did not take her online lessons today. Her school in the West Bank has declared this an official holiday. Years later, I wonder, will this day be a commemorative holiday in all schools and government ministries: a moment to celebrate victory, liberation, or salvation? And speaking of 'government', who will rule Gaza when the deal is completed, the prisoners exchanged and our cities rebuilt from dirt?

All I know is that today is Palestinian. Today Palestinians are celebrating everywhere: in Egypt, Jordan, Turkey, the Gulf,

America, Canada, even Norway. Everyone is distributing sweets to passersby.

I go to the hairdresser, despite the difficult circumstances and the dangers of walking in the streets. The occupation usually intensifies its raids just before a truce comes into effect so I'm surprised by the sight of five brides, each waiting their turn, along with fifteen other women here, to dye their hair in preparation for the truce. When women gather in one place, the conversation flows differently. I'm reminded how women in my country have better skills than men when it comes to political analysis and predictions.

The main focus of discussion is about the things we will do once the ceasefire comes into effect. The list of overheard wishes is long:

1. We will say goodbye to the endless queues at bakeries.
2. We will have electricity.
3. We will get rid of the monopoly of merchants.
4. We will be relieved from the high prices of basic resources.
5. We will free ourselves from prayer clothes as an official uniform during war.
6. We will replace our worn-out bank notes.
7. We will stop walking long distances and instead go back to putting up with the arrogant taxi driver who annoys us with his heroic stories about securing diesel during the war. His fare will become two shekels instead of seven.
8. We will solve the problem of slow internet.
9. I will embrace air conditioning in the summer.
10. We will say goodbye to firewood, embers, grease and lung conditions, and welcome the return of gas.
11. We will smoke cigarettes and shisha again, and be spared from all the cursing in our streets as a consequence.
12. We will eat meat, chicken, shawarma, maftoul, eggs, fresh vegetables, juices and ice cream.

13. I will kiss my husband; I miss our moments together.

14. Our children will return to school and to discipline.

15. Families will reunite, the South will join the North and we will see our loved ones again.

16. We will go back to drinking high-quality coffee, sold for fourteen shekels instead of 60.

17. We will no longer be devoured by drones, the quadcopter will be out of our lives.

18. We will mourn the martyrs and the missing with honour and dignity.

19. We will go back to walking in the streets without fear of shrapnel, or fear of going out and never coming back.

20. We will eat grilled corn on the promenade.

21. We will bathe under a shower.

22. We will light the streets at night.

23. We will stop following the news; in fact, one of the women offers to donate her TV.

24. We will go back to washing machines instead of hand washing.

25. I will bury my son, who remains under the rubble of the house.

January 17, 2025

I've been saving some canned lamb for over two weeks, waiting for a special occasion. It seems this day has finally arrived The gas cylinder we've been living off has been spluttering its last breaths for some time now; by tomorrow, it will be exhausted. We still have a few days before the aid lorries will start to enter Gaza, loaded with everything we have been deprived of: fuel, gas, food. The maps will change from now on, but I am ready to say goodbye to this life and welcome a new day for Gaza without war, even if it means concessions and change.

But where, then, will Habiba and I go? My own house is just rubble now. So it seems a new kind of evacuation awaits us. Should we emigrate and start a new life from scratch? Or should we stay here and rebuild everything from the ground up?

They are similar choices.

Some are speculating that, after reconstruction, the quality of life in Gaza will improve. Maybe so. But Gaza will remain a conflict zone, and we will still not enjoy real calm. Plus, what will happen to my job, helping displaced people in schools and shelters, when they return to their own areas? Even peace carries a thousand questions.

As for the empty neighbourhood around me...who knows how the population will shift again. Will the people in the South return to the North? Or will the people in the North want to leave these ruined cities? What about the fishing business? What about the border crossings? What about the thousands lucky enough to have been able to flee the Strip? Will they remain scattered around the world? What will happen to the makeshift markets that have sprung up? The goods, the banks, the daily transactions? Nothing is certain.

Will Gaza enter the privileged group of so-called 'developed' countries, or will we remain one of the eternally 'developing' ones? Will we invent new housing solutions to fit our reality — houses made of wood and cork that don't kill us when they're bombed — or will we be satisfied with open spaces and tents, without sustainable construction?

Oh God, I have discovered that adapting to war is easier than planning for what follows. Everything feels impossible, incomprehensible, as if a brand new conflict is beginning to take shape. This will be a war between the lines: invisible, unspoken. Are we ready to fight this new type of battle? Are we prepared to accept that the war we thought was over really isn't?

January 26, 2025

CHOCOLATE ENTERS GAZA

We have no displaced people to train. The residents of Beit Hanoun, Beit Lahia and Jabalia have returned to their homes, or what remains of them. These schools, which have seen so much overcrowding, are now almost empty.

Today, I see a man eating yellow-wrapped chocolates. At first, I think that it's just my imagination — a hallucination born of intense longing — but moments later, I see a child holding the same yellow bag: lifting it, and tipping all the chocolates into his mouth at once. A momentous event has occurred. The stalls on both sides of the road are selling chocolate, fizzy drinks and crisps! This is the best news for Gazans, even better than the ceasefire.

January 27, 2025

THE SEASON OF RETURNING TO THE NORTH

The miracle we thought would never happen has begun to occur. Hundreds of displaced families are arriving through the Netzarim Crossing, permitted to cross in accordance with the terms of the truce.

The young hold children on their shoulders, while carrying their belongings — food and drink boxes, woollen blankets, drums, flags, even tambourines — in their hands. The elderly lean on their grandchildren for support, carrying only their patience, and the fatigue of their years.

Men's backs are bent, and women's faces are marked by wrinkles. They've lived through months of sunshine, of standing in line for water, of standing in line for bread, of standing in line for aid.

Many have their tents with them — shelters which have almost become a part of their skin and bones, crumbling fortresses which have protected them from cold winter nights and blazing summer days. They cursed the pegs of these tents before dismantling them, but they couldn't leave them behind; these tents may still be their only refuge in the catastrophe of the North, amid tonnes of rubble, shattered glass and scattered iron rods. Still, the people of the South arrive with broad smiles and hearts filled with hope — some prostrate themselves on the land in gratitude. Some sing, some run and others jog. They all say, unanimously, 'It's my heart that's running, not my feet.'

Relatives, loved ones, friends and neighbours greet the returning masses, offering bottles of water, wreaths of flowers and Palestinian flags.

Here is a young man, welcoming his mother after a year and a half of separation.

Here is a little girl, reuniting with her father.

And here is a woman, arriving alone; her husband and son were martyred in the South, but she remains, she returns.

For me, I can't believe my brother and sister will be among us again soon, that we'll return to our long-yearned-for conversations over morning coffee.

If my grandparents could witness this scene, they would be overjoyed. We have succeeded where Palestinians have failed since 1948. Generations have learned from our ancestors' lessons and sworn to never abandon our land. The occupation's plans have failed. The great rift they created has been repaired. It was a long fifteen months, indeed, the longest period of our lifetimes. But the time has come for reunion. The aroma of coffee wafts, and we gather around the dining table to recount endless stories and anecdotes. Each of us has had our share of this devastating war.

Gaza is making its first return.

There will be no second Nakba.

January 28, 2025

Yesterday, we welcomed the return of our uncle and his family. Today, we welcome my eldest brother, Nazir, who we haven't seen since the beginning of the war. It is a majestic scene, enough to make the sky cry.

Companies have begun advertising their services in removing rubble, in cleaning homes with disinfectant, in installing nylon windows — all with the promise of specialised hands and highly experienced technicians. War breeds endless adaptability; endless enterprise.

Raghda, my uncle Abul Rahim's wife, tells us that she suspects every cup of tea she drinks in the North has been boiled on the embers of their stolen furniture. Their home was completely destroyed in the early days of the war, and after the building collapsed, thieves came to take her furniture and sell its wood by the kilo in the markets, where it burned beneath coffee cans, tea coolers and teapots throughout the genocide.

February 9, 2025

THE NETZARIM CORRIDOR REMOVED FOREVER

This morning, the Netzarim Corridor was removed; the occupation forces withdrew from it completely.

March 2, 2025

WAITING ON THE SIDELINES OF WAR

I've lost my job.

UNICEF services in Gaza have been suspended, the displacement map has changed and the psychological support programmes for children have ended. But I don't have the luxury of stopping or resting. Life in Gaza today has become a simple equation: those who don't work, don't breathe, don't eat, don't live. Thus begins my search for a new job, amid the exorbitant prices that make everything seem like a luxury.

Thankfully, today, I've received a text message inviting me to a job interview inside a school tent. Something was painful about the detail of the notification: the fact that recruitment procedures, once formal and orderly, have transformed into brief messages sent in a rush, without even the courtesy of a phone call.

I have promised my daughter Habiba a visit to a mall for Ramadan shopping. Seeing the density of the queues, I realise that Israel's closure of the Kerem Shalom Crossing [through which the occupation controls the entry of aid and supplies into Gaza] has once again raised the spectre of famine. Even in this ceasefire, it feels as if the enemy is slowly tightening the noose, as it always does and always has done, turning everything into a battle, even the basics of living.

March 3, 2025

SUHOOR PACKAGES AND CHANGING PRIORITIES

Today, I received another message, informing me of the need to pick up my suhoor package. A package containing qamar al-din [an apricot drink popular during Ramadan], cheese, jam and cookies is no trivial matter, but for me it is another reminder of how our priorities have shifted: from work, to aid packages; from dreams of a sumptuous meal to wondering when a gas cylinder will run out.

In Gaza, the small details of life remain silent daily battles.

March 6, 2025

A NEW JOB AND CONTINUING CONCERNS

Yesterday, I received a letter of acceptance for a position as a drama coach for girls at the Islamic University! Ironically, the news came in the same hasty manner as the interview request: no phone call, no formality, just a text message. Nevertheless, other things are on my mind: my daughter's schooling, stocking the fridge, planning for Mother's Day and dealing with a never-ending list of needs.

Despite everything, Habiba and I have decided to go out tonight to experience, once again, the pleasure of sitting at the recently reopened CUPRESSO Café in the middle of al-Rimal neighbourhood. Outside, children light up the night with fire-crackers made from steel wool, trailing sparks to create halos in the darkness, just as we did as children. These brief moments are enough to remind me that we are still alive, despite everything.

March 20, 2025

THE LAST GASP: THE WAR RETURNS

Gaza doesn't let you enjoy a moment of calm for long. Two days ago, shortly before suhoor, we woke to the sound of rockets and explosions. The truce had been violated, and death had returned. The occupation targeted many locations simultaneously, claiming hundreds of martyrs in a single night of bombing.

Work stopped.

School stopped.

We returned to analysis and newscasts; to tension and fear.

Today, on the twentieth day of Ramadan, the Israeli Army officially announced the return of ground operations in Northern Gaza. Sugar and gas supplies have been cut off, and the price of a cigarette has jumped to 50 shekels. The open door of Ramadan has closed on the resumption of war. The voices of children carry a familiar trace of fear.

NOTES

1. Over two million Palestinian Arabs, roughly one fifth of Israel's population, live within the current state of Israel, mainly concentrated in Arab-majority towns and cities such as Umm al-Fahm.

2. Israeli forces bombed Saint Porphyrius Greek Orthodox Church on October 19, 2023, killing eighteen of the people sheltering there, including a three-month-old baby.

3. Israeli forces besieged al-Shifa for a second time between March 18 and April 1, 2024, killing, injuring or detaining 1500 people, and reducing much of the hospital to rubble. Reporting for *Mondoweiss*, the Palestinian journalist Tareq S. Hajjaj interviewed many survivors of the siege, detailing the occupation's horrific violence including mass executions, the murder of medical workers and the shootings of at least 22 patients in their beds. Following the massacre, an IDF spokesperson described the military operation as 'one of the most successful of the war so far'.

4. Mahmoud Darwish's poem, from his collection *Why Did You Leave The Horse Alone* (1995), describes a father and child, forcibly displaced, who leave a horse behind to watch over their abandoned home: 'Why did you leave the horse alone? / —To keep the house company, my son / For houses die when their inhabitants leave.'

5. Hanzala: The cartoon depiction of a young boy with his back turned, created by the artist Naji al-Ali as a symbol of Palestinian displacement, resistance and eventual return. It is said that Hanzala will only turn to face us when the occupation of Palestine ends.

6. On May 7, 2025, Israeli drones simultaneously struck the Thailandy Restaurant and a nearby market stall, killing 33 Palestinians according to the BBC. Among those murdered in the Thailandy Restaurant attack was the journalist Yahya Sobeih, whose daughter had been born just hours earlier.

7. Al-Aqsa Mosque: the third holiest site in Islam is located in Occupied East Jerusalem.

8. Yahya Sinwar: de facto leader of Hamas following the assassination of Ismail Haniyeh on July 31, 2024 (see Nahil's entry for August 1, 2024). Sinwar was killed in a clash with Israeli forces on October 16, 2024. Israeli drone footage, later released by the IDF, shows Sinwar's final moments: mortally wounded, and using the last of his strength to throw a stick at the watching camera.

9. Hassan Nasrallah: the Secretary General of Hezbollah, assassinated by Israeli airstrike in Beirut, Lebanon, on September 24, 2024.

Ala'a Obaid

ALA'A OBAID is a writer and a mother of three children. She has held a number of positions in various NGOs and cultural institutions in Gaza, including Education Officer, Creative Writing Teacher and Culture Centre Coordinator. Ala'a co-authored the books *Writing Behind the Lines* and *Disturbing Flashbacks*, both of which document the experiences of Palestinians living through the current genocide. She has published several articles in *The New Arab*. Excerpts from her diaries have been performed by Hind Shoufani at the Barbican Theatre, London, and by Zarah Sultana MP at the Belgrade Theatre, Coventry.

To my child Ibrahim, who came into this world on Valentine's Day 2024, in spite of this war.

AT 5:30AM THIS MORNING, my brother Jamil's gentle voice interrupted my sleep, telling me an evacuation order had been issued for Gaza City and the northern areas of the Strip; telling me that the international organisations were already packing up. The news didn't stir anything in me. I drifted back to sleep as if I hadn't heard.

It wasn't till 7am that the sound of movement on the staircase of our building jolted me into consciousness. Before I knew it, I was wearing my headscarf and halfway to my grandfather's apartment on the ground floor. There, I found my Uncle Ziad, along with my uncles-through-marriage Mohammad and Bashar, all clutching their phones anxiously and reading aloud the names of friends and acquaintances who might host them in the South.

My father entered with sarcasm and suppressed anger in his eyes — emotions I have rarely seen him display. From the moment the talk of displacement began, I knew my father would never leave.

Indeed, in a tone that carried deep reproach for anyone planning to flee, my father asked: 'Why should we abandon our home? What will they do? They just want to isolate the city.'

My uncle tried to convince him otherwise, arguing that this war is particularly vicious, that the unknown is terrifying and that my grandmother's limited mobility will make it impossible to escape if a sudden bombing occurs.

Later, in my parents' apartment on the second floor, my father sat on his bed, his face flushed with rage.

I begged him to reconsider his decision, but he snapped, 'I've heard your opinion, thank you. I don't need to hear more. What you do is up to you. I won't force anyone to stay.'

I left the room and began to cry. I was in no state for another confrontation. Vivid and violent images of the future raced through my mind: scenes of random shelling as I held my screaming children Basil (age six) and Rusal (age four), running from death to death as poisonous gas filled our skies.

I packed my things and called my husband, Nemer, telling him I'd decided to leave. Soon, Nemer arrived at my parents' house, carrying more clothes, our passports, wedding photos and important documents. We drove south, caught in the crush of cars. I was shocked by the destruction in the city — entire neighbourhoods wiped out by bombing; people carrying their belongings, fleeing in fear. We crossed Wadi Gaza on the coastal road; the traffic stretched out for miles ahead.

At every junction, someone told us, 'You won't get through, it's packed.'

The 30-minute trip turned into a four-hour ordeal.

When we finally reached my sister, Sarah, at the Hamad City Apartment Complex in Khan Younis, I hugged her and burst into tears. The moment shattered me. The pain was unbearable, my chest tight with sorrow.

Later, we learnt that the occupation had bombed a convoy of evacuees on the same road we'd travelled on, shortly after we'd passed. 70 people were killed in that strike alone.

October 18, 2023

Our first few days in Hamad passed in cautious quiet, less terrifying than hearing the blasts of airstrikes in Gaza City.

On the fifth day of our stay, my uncle Ziad called. He wanted us to take in another twenty people: his brothers and their families. Our number swelled to 35 people in one small apartment. Perhaps surprisingly, we were comforted by the crowd. There's a feeling of safety in numbers, though it's an illusion, of course.

Last night the discussion began: where would all these people sleep in a 110-square-metre apartment? It was suggested that the young men move to the guard's room, downstairs. I don't know how the discussion ended, but eventually everyone agreed to sleep in the main living room.

Moments later, news hit us like thunder: an Israeli airstrike on al-Ahli Baptist Hospital.[1] A hospital! What is happening to this world?

I dozed off, with pain and sorrow twisting in my chest, then jolted awake to the sound of two explosions, the second so violent I thought the building was collapsing in on us. I recited the Shahada over and over, trembling with fear as the wail of sirens and neighbours' screams filled the air. I heard a woman wailing from the depths of her soul. I grabbed my phone and started recording, feeling certain I would one day write her story.

Fifteen people were killed in that strike: buried in their beds, their sleep becoming permanent. The rubble had crushed a little girl's face. Her name, like that of my sister, was Sarah. She was six years old; not the youngest or oldest of her siblings, but the dearest to her parents, their precious miracle after a difficult pregnancy.

Her mother cried endlessly, repeating, 'I wish I hadn't put her to bed early. I wish...'

This morning, everyone began searching for new shelters. We all considered places that might be 'safer', though nowhere truly is. My uncle Ziad decided to go to a house in al-Qarara; my sister Sarah to her in-laws in al-Dahra; my mother and my uncle's wife to Gaza City.

After lots of thought, my husband Nemer and I decided to go to a second shelter in Khan Younis, though Nemer preferred the idea of returning to Gaza City. Every departing family embraced and wept, knowing we might never see each other again.

The road to the shelter was long, and full of people asking for and giving directions. When we finally arrived, I was shocked by the volume of tents and people. I headed to the shelter's administration office and joined a long queue. A piece of paper was taped to the wall, reading:

'Shelter full. Please proceed to the following schools...'

Another note, whose words I don't remember exactly, warned of heavy rain which could damage the shelter. I returned to the car and reported this to Nemer, then sat for a moment, torn between going to a school and heading to al-Qarara, just north of Khan Younis.

Nemer seemed to sense my indecision. Without discussion, he floored the accelerator and said, 'We're going back to Gaza City. There's no other choice.'

Returning to my parents' home, I felt a deep ache, a crushing sorrow and a fear I'd never experienced before. I was pale, tearful, unable to eat.

My mother asked, 'What's wrong, my love?'

I lay beside her and melted into her embrace.

'Cry, if you need to,' she said gently.

So I cried.

Tonight is among the quietest since the war began but I can't sleep. My eyes refuse to rest. I am five months pregnant. The air smells of gas. It feels as though the baby inside me has stopped moving.

October 19, 2023

This morning, I made my decision: I would head south again. I told myself that I had to do everything in my power to protect my children. The bombing, the scent of gunpowder and the phosphorus hanging in the sky were threatening the life of the foetus growing inside me. I couldn't bear the guilt of losing it.

I decided to join my uncle in al-Qarara, just north of Khan Younis, even if it meant evacuating alone. Yes, this was a desperate attempt to grasp at anything remotely reassuring, to escape an uncertain fate which gnashes its teeth at us with every passing moment.

First, I headed to al-Shifa Hospital, to the maternity ward, stumbling over the dozens of women and children asleep on the floor before finally reaching the exam room, where I asked to see a doctor. I was scared for my baby.

Somebody asked, 'Where are you from? Don't you know we're in crisis mode? We only see bleeding cases.'

I didn't respond.

After a moment, he said, 'Lie down, I'll check the heartbeat.'

My baby was OK, thank God.

In the meantime, Nemer had found a driver willing to travel to Khan Younis. I managed to roll a mattress into the car's boot, along with two thermal blankets from my sister Sarah's apartment, then I climbed into the crowded car with my children, Basil and Rusal — all of us wedged between four girls on the back seat. I smiled at Nemer as we waved him goodbye. Inside, my stomach was churning.

As the car headed south, we passed through what remained of our city: abandoned, lifeless. The buildings looked like diminished old women: bent and ready to collapse. We had barely reached the edge of al-Zaytoun neighbourhood when a massive explosion erupted just metres in front of us. Smoke rose thick and dark and all of us screamed, reciting the Shahada again. I held onto Basil and Rusal and shut my eyes. If this was the end, I didn't want to see it.

One of the girls shouted, 'Go! Follow the car that just passed!'

The driver stepped hard on the accelerator. Our speed reached over 60 miles per hour. Somehow we made it through.

Now, we are staying in al-Qarara, in a building previously empty for fifteen years. No water, no electricity, no mattresses; only a bare structure. This building belongs to a relative of Abu Jalal, a friend of my uncle Ziad. Abu Jalal lives in a neat villa halfway along Salah al-Din Road. His relatives, the owners of this building, migrated to Europe years ago.

Al-Qarara is farmland covered in orange trees. Our building stands in the middle of these trees. It has four floors, but all the apartments are locked except for the this one, which is open-plan, with no partitions and no privacy for anyone. One bathroom serves 30 people.

I am lying with my children on two thin, worn-out mattresses; little better than lying directly on the floor. Lying like this, while pregnant, is extremely painful.

Questions flood my mind.

Oh God, how long will I remain here?

October 21, 2023

Today, I receive a message from my colleague Layali, a psychologist at the Rasel Centre for Creativity on al-Wadha Street. I am the centre's coordinator, and we have worked together for four years, sharing bread, salt and occasional disagreements.

Layali's message reads: 'Alhamdulillah. We are exhausted, Ala'a. We have no energy left. The news of Nada's martyrdom has broken our hearts. May God have mercy on her.'

I can't believe it.

I reply: 'You mean Hiba Abu Nada?[2] What happened to her?'

Layali, realising I haven't heard the bad news, chooses not to answer.

There is no internet. Even regular messages barely get through. I'm afraid I'll lose many friends while isolated like this.

Hiba — bright, eloquent, talented — was a gifted writer and a passionate dreamer. She led the Science and Engineering Club at the Rasel Centre. How could death steal her passion for life so swiftly?

Just two days before the war, Hiba and I were chatting on WhatsApp, excited to revive the Rasel Centre's programme for gifted students. She had been eager, full of ambition, ready to continue our mission. Often, on work mornings, she'd share her dreams of travel — telling me how border closures had left her unable to physically receive the Sharjah Award for her novel *Oxygen Is Not for the Dead*.

In Hiba, I saw someone desperate to knock on life's doors, explore new cities, meet new people and quench her thirst for experience. But oxygen has run out for both the living and the dead.

I finally find internet access, at the top of Salah al-Din Road, and post a tribute to Hiba on the Rasel Centre's Facebook page. I look at each photo of her closely. In every image she's explaining, smiling, thinking, asking, debating.

Hiba, remember when I told you once that our work at Rasel is continuous: always sharing knowledge that benefits others? My consolation is that you've left behind a legacy, one that will elevate your soul and stature through the minds of the people you nurtured.

Rest in peace, habibti.

October 29, 2023

I tell my uncle I want to go to the market to buy autumn clothes for my children; their summer clothes are no longer enough for the cold evenings.

On my way back, I visit the 'Family Mall' on Salah al-Din Road. Following the outbreak of war, its owner hung a huge sign that read: *al-Faraj* [place of relief]. This was a thoughtful gesture: the new name fits the harshness of our reality. Everyone here seeks relief, waits for it, prays for it.

Inside the mall, I notice that chocolate, snacks and everything else have nearly sold out. I dare to ask for the wi-fi password. The generous owner doesn't hesitate to supply it.

On Facebook, I see a new post: 'Why did you leave us, my dear Meryam?'

Meryam Kabaja! But how?

Meryam's aunt is in mourning. In her post, she explains that an Israeli missile struck the house next to Meryam's, near al-Shati Camp. The shrapnel tore through Meryam's body and the bodies of her children, martyring them instantly. Seconds before the bombing, Meryam and her two daughters had gone upstairs. Her loving husband remained downstairs, waiting for them to come back. But they didn't. And they won't.

Meryam Kabaja was a laboratory technician, loved for her bright face, gentle accent and warm humour. I remember telling a friend that Meryam would make a great match for her brother. Not long afterwards: Meryam and my friend's brother did indeed get married. Even though this was the first advice I'd ever given on a marriage proposal, my sisters Sarah and Asmaa teased me relentlessly.

'Ala'a: The Matchmaking Society,' they joked. 'Ala'a: Blessed and Hitched.'

Can you believe it? A family formed just a few years ago: shattered by the press of a button.

October 30, 2023

Here, in al-Qarara, I suffered my first family loss of this war. Just over a week ago, my maternal grandmother, Umm Adnan, passed away suddenly. She wasn't ill. She had no complaints. She was simply sleeping in my aunt Sanaa's house when her hands went limp, her face turned pale and her soul ascended to its creator. She'd suffered a sudden heart attack.

When I heard the news, I cried alone. I longed to hug my mother, to be by her side in her grief.

My aunt Suad tried to console me: 'Umm Adnan had someone to bury her. Pray that when we die, we find someone to bury us.' By now, hundreds have been martyred. Many bodies remain unrecovered: one pain atop another.

I sit under an orange tree, remembering my grandmother: her presence, her dignity, the way people revered her. I remember how, in my childhood, my mother would rarely show me approval, except when my grandmother praised me. I learnt to please my mother by pleasing my grandmother. I'd sweep the front garden, water the plants and buy fava beans and falafel from Zahran's shop.

My mother used to say, 'Parents are like the scent of roses in this world. Let me cherish them while I can, before they disappear.'

My grandmother left with no goodbye; I didn't get to kiss her forehead. My displacement prevents me from hugging my mother. We can't share our loss.

I am becoming accustomed to this life of displacement. I have learnt what it means to bathe using a single kettle of water, and only when water and firewood are available. I have learnt to cook over an open flame. I have learnt to wash clothes by hand, not wasting a drop of the water we have.

Every morning brings the struggle of securing a loaf of bread. Above all, the deafening sound of explosions never ceases.

November 12, 2023

Yesterday, fifteen members of my family — including my father Imad, my youngest brother Mohammad, my aunt Jihad and Jihad's children — found themselves under siege in my aunt Jihad's home in Gaza City.

Sounds of shelling surrounded them on all sides, followed by a cascade of gunfire. The Israeli tanks had withdrawn from the front of al-Shifa Hospital only to station themselves in front of my father's house on Hamid Street.

My father, brother, aunt and cousins had no internet access, and no way of knowing what was happening outside. But we did. Along with my sisters and my mother (who has finally joined us in the South), I was glued to my phone, feeling that every passing minute was more perilous than the last.

From a distance, we launched emergency appeals and contacted satellite TV channels, hoping to save our family's lives. We tried calling the Red Cross, but it was Saturday, and few Red Cross staff were working. Those we managed to reach apologised, saying they couldn't help due to the intensity of the shelling and the inaccessibility of the area.

One of my cousin's colleagues launched a plea in both Arabic and English, which spread like wildfire across social media, restoring our hope.

This morning, a rocket injured two members of my besieged family. Shrapnel crashed through a window and pierced the chest of my younger cousin Hadeel, while her sister Majd's husband suffered a deep shrapnel wound to his leg.

My father and those trapped with him were about to leave when they received the news that Jihad's sister-in-law Hala, a woman in her sixties, has been shot in the head by Israeli forces after stepping out of a nearby house.

Everything has gone silent. Is death finally here, knocking at our door? Can human life be this cheap?

I close my eyes in pain.

November 13, 2023

This morning, the Red Cross finally coordinated an evacuation. My father, brother and the entire group of fifteen family members set out as instructed: abandoning their possessions and heading east towards al-Wahda Street, carrying only a white flag. Yet as soon as they reached al-Shifa intersection, heavy gunfire rained down on them.

My father decided to turn back, terrified.

My brother Mohammad cried, and begged him, 'We can't go back! They'll kill us if we return.'

Bullets were flying past, one even piercing their white flag. They ran like characters in a PUBG game.[3] At every intersection, the Israeli Army seemed to deliberately target them. The whole thing felt like a brutal, unfair trap.

November 15, 2023

On the night of November 13, my father and those fleeing with him took refuge in al-Shawa Square, in a house belonging to relatives, waiting for the 'safe hours', before traveling further south. During the night, a shell landed on a neighbouring house, causing my father to suffer shortness of breath and a spike in blood pressure. Fortunately, my aunt Jihad procured a sedative from a nearby pharmacy, and managed to administer it successfully.

This morning, my father's party continued their evacuation via the so-called 'safe corridor,' following the occupation's instructions. As I would later learn, they had reached the Kuwait Roundabout and started walking south when an Israeli Army loudspeaker suddenly blared: 'The man in white trousers and the man behind him, stop for inspection.'

My 60-year-old father and my beautiful twenty-year-old brother Mohammad were taken to an Israeli detention camp. The camp held dozens of detainees, including women and children. An army officer started asking for IDs, then began calling names one by one — giving some permission to leave, taking others for interrogation.

My father sat in a spot from which he could see the initial inspection area. He watched as an Israeli soldier, speaking Arabic, gave orders to a young Palestinian man: 'Give me your mobile phone and all your belongings…Now take off your clothes and shoes.'

At 2pm, an officer called my brother Mohammad's name and told him to proceed to interrogation. Like the others before him, Mohammad was stripped, blindfolded, handcuffed and led away — vanishing behind the sand dunes as my father watched, unable to help.

Meanwhile, in our place of relative safety, we were praying for our father and brother, without knowing what had happened to them. We were counting the minutes until their arrival.

Then came a shocking WhatsApp message from my uncle: 'The occupation has detained your father and brother.'

My mother lost all balance. Her face turned pale and her body trembled, as if in agony. Mohammad, her youngest, the joy of her heart! My sisters feared we might lose her from the shock and grief.

I held her tightly, begging her to stay strong: 'They'll come back soon, Mama. It's just questioning. It will only take an hour. We'll see them again.'

Then I went into the bathroom and cried until I couldn't breathe. This pain is unbearable.

It was 3pm…4pm. We all watched the clock. Some detainees were released, we heard news of their arrival, but my father and brother weren't among them.

At 5pm, darkness fell. We never stopped praying, never stopped pleading until, finally, a message arrived on my mother's phone. My father was trying to call.

We fell into prostration, weeping with gratitude and joy. Everything around us seemed to change — hope, almost vanished, suddenly returned.

But then, amid the celebratory cries of 'Alhamdulillah' [praise be to God], came the chilling words of my sister Asmaa's husband: 'Only your father has been released, the Israelis are still detaining your brother.'

His voice silenced everything.

Now, grief has robbed us of our momentary joy.

November 20, 2023

My youngest brother Mohammad still hasn't appeared.

My older brother Jamil has begun going to the Netzarim Checkpoint every day, waiting from 10am to 4pm for any news of him.

I've tried contacting journalist friends. After connecting with colleagues in the West Bank, I was able to speak to a Red Cross officer named Abie. He filled out a form detailing every aspect of Mohammad's abduction.

He told me, 'Maybe in two weeks we'll know something,' adding, 'I feel your pain, and I'm truly sorry.'

Mohammad loves wearing white. He's a great photographer. He has a wonderful sense of humour and is arguably the most handsome young man in our family. He expresses love better than anyone.

'My dear, I swear I missed you.' This is how Mohammad always welcomes me, along with a long hug. We've often sat together, enjoying a cup of coffee and exchanging funny stories, hours passing as if they were minutes.

Before the genocide, whenever I visited my parents, Mohammad would postpone all his plans and outings just to spend time with me.

I used to tell him: 'Go run your errands.'

And he would reply, 'No, you're more important.'

I remember when my daughter Rusal fractured her arm and the doctors told us she needed surgery. Mohammad came straight to the hospital, running to meet me.

He whispered: 'She's going to be OK.'

The moment he embraced me, I broke down in tears. And he cried with me.

From Mohammad, I learnt to tell those I love that I love them. From Mohammad, I learnt to create moments of love with those I hold dear.

Dearest Mohammad, your story isn't over yet.

December 7, 2023

On December 2, the day after war resumed [following a six-day truce], we woke to the sound of an explosion. Along with my family, I'd returned to my sister Sarah's apartment in Hamad City. A neighbouring tower had been bombed and two martyrs were soon announced.

Time passed slowly. The sound of Hamad City seemed louder than usual. We felt something was wrong. Then my brother Jamil told us the Israelis had divided the Gaza Strip into more than 600 numbered blocks, and instructed Gazans to learn their block numbers, in preparation for evacuation.

At the same time, my sister Sarah received an email from one of the international organisations, it contained a military instruction telling people to evacuate Block 37: the block containing Hamad City!

Worry crept into our hearts, though we tried to brush it off, saying, 'They won't bomb all of Hamad City. Maybe just individual apartments.'

Moments later: two explosions. The children began to scream. The building shook violently, threatening to collapse around us.

A third explosion.

We fled in chaos, then gathered in a doorway, clinging to each other. We were sure the bombing wouldn't stop.

A fourth, a fifth explosion.

The nearby towers had been struck. Everyone started crying and screaming. Those were excruciating moments; we realised that our life in Hamad City was over, that we would be displaced once again.

In the silence that followed the airstrikes, each of us began to pack our belongings. This time, we only packed essential winter clothes, bedding and blankets. We left our summer clothes behind, we had no need for them. The seasons had changed; the war remained.

We didn't leave together.

'It's better to divide the burden,' my mother said.

And so it was: she and my father left to find shelter in the tents at al-Sinaa; my sisters, Asmaa and Sarah, left to stay with my aunt Sanaa in al-Dahra Camp in Khan Younis; and my brother Jamil, his wife Sarah, and I left to seek shelter in a private kindergarten in Tel al-Sultan, in Rafah.

I hugged my mother goodbye, choking on tears at the thought of another separation.

I arrived at the kindergarten full of nerves. Although Jamil's in-laws had arrived ahead of us, this was my first time staying among so many strangers. But as soon as I entered, I was surrounded by kind people who embraced me like family.

What stood out most was the emotional bond among the families: their optimism and humour in defiance of the harshness of war and daily life. Most of them had lost their homes, yet they still tried to smile, in spite of everything.

But there was suffering too, especially in the challenge of providing enough food for the growing number of displaced people. More families were arriving, relatives of those already staying there. Like me, they had fled Khan Younis and Hamad City as the bombardment intensified in the South.

Soon, we were over 70 people.

Two days ago, at sunset, we were startled by a group of young men trying to break into the kindergarten. They were local residents, believing they had a greater right than we had to use the shelter. The noise outside grew frightening. Rusal and Basil clung to me tightly. In war, people run out of patience. Conflict and dispute become ever-present options, often erupting over the simplest things, especially in places like Tel al-Sultan, where tents had spread across the pavements and streets.

The dispute ended with an agreement: two rooms of the kindergarten would be cleared for new displaced families. But these rooms were barely enough for the current residents — how could we possibly make room for more?

December 9, 2023

Yesterday, I came to visit my parents. After a few days in a tent in al-Sinaa, my uncles arranged for them to live in this rented apartment here in Rafah.

I told my father what I'd experienced at the kindergarten and he insisted I stay here instead of returning. So my children and I have moved in with my parents, raising the number of displaced people in this apartment to over 40.

The apartment faces the sea directly. Last night, Israeli naval boats fired shells into the Strip, their cannons so loud we felt the shells were aimed at us.

'O God, where are we supposed to go?' I whispered.

'Mama, will the war last long?' my daughter Rusal asked.

I answered nervously, using my usual line to comfort her: 'Just two more days, then it'll be over.'

This lie was all I had.

Today, Basil begged me to let him and Rusal collect seashells on the beach — something he'd watched the other children doing yesterday. I didn't like the idea. But after some back and forth, I agreed.

As my children search the beach, I sit facing the sea, contemplating the past, the present, the future. I make many wishes, all wrapped up in the same three words: survive, heal, forget.

I stare at the Israeli gunboat, still floating in front of us. Its presence doesn't scare me any more, not even its proximity to the shore. We've become accustomed to our fates.

What pains me most is how seemlessly the sound of the waves blends with the roar of an Israeli F-16 flying overhead. Even this sea, into which we've poured so many of our sorrows, is conspiring with the machines sent to kill us.

My children's laughter rings out, celebrating the big bag of seashells they've gathered. It's the most beautiful sound.

January 2, 2024

This morning we woke to the sound of screaming: 'Mohammad is out of prison! He called cousin Faraj! He's at the Kerem Shalom Crossing!'

We were stunned.

We cried.

We cheered.

Here was the news we had awaited for 49 days: 49 days filled with every colour of pain and loss.

My father and uncles go to meet Mohammad, while we stand in the street, waiting. My mother weeps with joy as people come to congratulate us — some don't even know my brother, they are just happy to know that someone has been set free.

A white car approaches. My mother waves. At last Mohammad emerges, his hair longer, his posture contorted. He hugs my mother. They cry together for a long time. Then I hug him too, with tears of joy in my eyes. Our family cheers, claps and holds Mohammad close — as if only physical touch will allow us to believe he has returned.

Mohammad: the youngest, the most beloved.

We prepare a feast, inviting friends, family and displaced people from nearby neighbourhoods. It's the happiest we've been in 90 days of war, and we steal the moment, celebrating every second. But doubt haunts me. I see the wounds on Mohammad's neck and hands. I fear he has been through horrors.

When the visitors leave, we form a circle around Mohammad, eager to hear his story. He tells us everything:

How he and the other detainees were taken off buses in the freezing cold and beaten under the rain.

How most of the detainees had no political affiliations, but were randomly kidnapped from the road.

How the severe torture during interrogations forced him to confess to things he hadn't done.

How the Israeli soldiers would convince themselves their detainees were killers or terrorists — allowing themselves to torture our men without remorse.

I look away, hiding my tears as my brother recounts how they'd locked him in a metal cage and set a vicious dog on him.

'Don't worry,' he says with a weak smile. 'The dog was trained to injure, not to kill. Besides, it's all behind me now. What matters is that I'm with you, and we're OK together.'

February 2, 2024

For days now, I've spent hours wandering through al-Awda market in Rafah, searching for clothes for my unborn baby.

When I left Gaza City, carrying a child who was not yet five months in my womb, I hadn't packed a bundle of baby clothes, nor had I chosen a name. My body hadn't fully rounded with his presence and I hadn't yet imagined his features. Nor had I imagined I would be giving birth to him in a war that stretched on for months and months.

Standing in the middle of the market, I have repeatedly turned in circles, scanning every corner, hoping to spot a sign offering 'Newborn Clothes'. My feet have led me nowhere, but each day I have clung to the hope that I might find something for the baby that's growing inside me.

Today, after a long search, I reach a store called Mansour [victorious], which I have been told is the largest baby clothing shop in Rafah. The moment I step inside, the shopkeeper glances at me, recognising the advanced stage of my pregnancy. His gaze carries something between pity and regret.

'Everything is gone,' he says. 'You're too late.'

I walk to another shop, but before I can even ask, the owner shakes his head. 'We have nothing left.'

In a third shop, the seller, after apologising, says, 'Don't exhaust yourself looking. The market is completely empty. Even in second-hand stalls, you won't find anything you're looking for.'

Then, a thought strikes me: I could buy fabric and take it to a tailor to sew some swaddles and baby clothes. I rush to find a tailor, and soon see one in a nearby street, surrounded by a crowd. Excitedly, I explain my plan. I even hint that I'll pay him well.

The tailor sighs. 'During war, tailoring is almost impossible. There's barely any electricity. I'm only here to patch up torn pairs of trousers.'

This evening, I receive a call from my sister Noor, who lives in Kuwait.

'My friend in Egypt is willing to buy everything you need,' she tells me, 'but we need to find someone to bring the clothes into Gaza.'

I immediately contact a friend living abroad, asking if she knows of anyone traveling to Gaza soon.

My friend hesitates before replying. 'Ala'a, who would travel to Gaza now?'

I'm due to give birth in a matter of weeks. What else can I do?

February 12, 2024

A week ago, I received an unexpected message from my friend Mona, checking in on me, praying for my safety and hoping we might meet again after the war. She finished her message with, 'If you need baby clothes, let me know. Most shops are closed, and there's barely any stock left.'

My mother went to a shop that sells curtain fabric, choosing a soft velvet material. She asked the seller to cut it into swaddles. Then she went to al-Sultan neighbourhood, where used clothes were scattered randomly on makeshift stalls.

Two days before my due date, she stumbled upon a street vendor selling white newborn undergarments. She bought them immediately, and threw each item into boiling water, stirring continuously to disinfect them as thoroughly as possible.

My uncle Ziad chuckled, watching her. 'This is how our grandmothers used to do it back in the old days.'

I'd given Mona my address so she could send the promised baby clothes. But days have passed, and nothing has arrived.

Today, she calls and apologises. 'The house next to mine was bombed five days ago. Rubble collapsed onto our house, we've been trying to clear it up.'

She swears she'll still find a way to save some clothes and bring them to me.

February 14, 2024

This morning, I opened my eyes and felt pain tearing through me. Tears came. I was going to give birth to my child as a displaced person, far away from home, far from my husband and far from all the small comforts a mother needs when her baby is coming.

I was exhausted and sad: afraid of everything that was coming. I wasn't confident in my ability to keep my baby safe. My womb has been safer than the brutally of this war.

My mother prepared the maternity supplies, and we headed together to the Emirati Hospital, the only hospital designated for maternity cases in the city of Rafah

At 9am, we began the screening procedures. Dozens of women stood in a long line, waiting for their initial examinations. My mother was upset about the number of cases and the time it would take for me to be seen. There was no bed for me in the hospital. The beds were for bleeding and serious cases only. I was instructed to walk around the hospital and return in two hours, but my pain increased with every minute, faster than I could bear.

After two hours, I went for my examination. The doctors told me to walk for another two hours. They suggested that I should go home and come back in the evening.

My mother refused: 'We live near the sea... the distance is too great... we won't be able to leave and return before nightfall... transportation is too hard to arrange.'

The doctor wasn't tactful in his speech; he reiterated that there were no beds in the hospital, that I wasn't in a serious condition, I wasn't bleeding and my foetus wasn't weak.

I couldn't believe that a hospital would refuse a maternity patient just because it was not a case of life and death. Have we really reached this point?

I cried profusely. My mother became emotional.

'My daughter is giving birth,' she told the doctor. 'She is in pain, unable to move. And you say there is no bed for her to lie on! This is unacceptable.'

The doctor began making excuses: blaming the war, the demands of emergency cases and anything else he could think of. He motioned for my mother to wait.

After a while, he returned, and said, 'I've found a bed for you.'

I was shown to a room containing four patients and an unusable ensuite bathroom. The doctor said I needed time; that I was looking at a four or five hour wait. He asked one of the nurses to put me on the foetus monitor and start a line. I lay on the bed — a bed with no sheets.

My mother left the room to get some food and drink and other supplies. But after only a few minutes had passed, I began to feel unbearable pain, and started calling out for her.

A porter was sitting next to me, and said, 'Your mother isn't here, but I'm here if you need anything.'

I motioned that I wanted to lean on her to go to the bathroom in the next room. As soon as I entered the bathroom, the pain reached a point I have never experienced in my life. I decided within myself that something bad had happened; that there had been a mistake in the diagnosis. This pain couldn't be labour, it had to be internal bleeding or a rupture in my uterus. I groaned and cried. The agony was unbearable

I shouted involuntarily.

The porter called back, 'Open the door!'

I tried to respond, terrified that I would lose my baby.

The porter rushed to fetch a female doctor from the hospital corridor. As soon as the doctor entered, she asked me to come with her.

I told her, 'I can't move. I am giving birth now; something bad is happening.'

She asked me again.

I answered her screaming, 'I can't!'

Then we saw my little baby falling to the floor, his first cry stunning everyone in the room. I had given birth to a child while standing!

I saw fear and panic flood the doctor's face. She asked me to lie on the floor immediately. She shouted for special equipment, and put the baby on my chest. I don't know why, but I didn't look at him, even though I was able to. I think I was afraid that if I saw him, if he was injured in any way, my heart would stop.

I requested he be put under observation for 24 hours. I requested an X-ray of his head and rib cage.

At that moment, my mother returned, turning pale from the horror of what she saw. She sat next to me on the floor, holding my hand and crying.

'May God protect the mother and the baby,' she prayed.

Minutes later, the doctor asked me to follow her to the delivery room, to stitch the wounds. She apologised that no wheelchair or portable bed was available.

As I walked, I heard another pregnant woman screaming in intense pain,'My love, may God gather me with you in paradise. O God, let me join the martyrs and prophets and my beloved.'

How many women in our country are having the children of men who have died in this war?

It's 10pm.

Someone has come to reassure me that my child is OK. He has survived. I have survived. Now, my newborn son, Ibrahim, is screaming his first sounds in a war that takes away all the colours of life.

The world should be ashamed of what is happening to us.

March 1, 2024

My friend Mona called while I was in the hospital.

'Mona, I gave birth just a few hours ago,' I told her.

The next day, February 16, she arrived with her sister Asia, congratulating me with a warm smile.

'Welcome to the world, little one,' Mona said, laughing. 'Ala'a, I had to take two taxis and a car just to get here!'

A week before the war started, Mona and I spent an evening together by the sea, laughing without a care in the world. That night was full of joy and noise. But now, every memory from before the war feels like a treasured relic, and hurts the heart to recall. So, during her visit, we spoke only about the hardship of labour, of endless displacement, of the struggle to survive.

As Mona was leaving, we shared a simple wish: 'Let's meet again in Gaza City when this war is over.'

I never imagined her hospital visit would be the last time I saw Mona. I never thought, when I walked Mona to the road, exchanging good wishes, that it was our final farewell. Had I known, I would have hugged her longer. I would have thanked her more. I would have told her how strong, loving and remarkable she was. I would have told her that her smile each morning was the most beautiful thing about her.

Yesterday, thirteen days after she brought me the baby clothes she had promised to deliver, Mona was killed. I saw her name by chance on the list of martyrs. Death had taken her and moved on.

After reading her name, I looked down at my newborn, my child of war: the baby who will one day be told, 'You were born during our displacement.'

Tears streamed down my face: tears for Mona, tears for my child, tears for the cruelty of it all.

May 5, 2024

The sound of commotion, clapping, cheering.

I rush to the window. Everyone is chanting: 'Truce… truce… truce!'

Children are running and dancing in the street. Celebratory gunfire echoes. Women ululate, embrace and congratulate each other for surviving. My seven-year-old son Basil runs towards me and hugs me, his cheeks flushed with joy.

'We're going back to Gaza, Mama,' he says. 'We'll see Baba [father], and I'll go back to the club and play football.' He goes on, excitedly, telling me everything he plans to do once the ceasefire begins.

Basil doesn't fully grasp the realities of war, but he lives in the joy of the moment completely. All of us cling to the same thread of hope: the promise that the rumours of a ceasefire carry.

Then the news begins to spread: Israel has rejected the truce. Everything shrinks. Joy fades. The city's noise subsides and I grow tired of my helplessness. I collapse into myself, exhausted.

I decide not to burden myself with more sorrow. I resolve that the war will only end when the living survive, the martyrs are buried and our loved ones return. Only then will we choose our corners to cry in.

I convince myself that the war will last several more months, preparing myself with harsh expectations, increasing my ability to endure. The days ahead will be painful; above all, they will require patience and resilience, especially with the looming threat of Rafah being stormed.[4]

May 7, 2024

Yesterday, we woke to the news that the Rafah Crossing had been invaded, and Israeli flags raised in its courtyards.

Today, I hear the noise of displacement, and step outside to see the crowds moving with all their belongings, heading towards...nothingness. Dozens of families are transporting what remains of their possessions on donkey carts, lorries and cars; fleeing the hell of war, following the instructions printed on the leaflets dropped by enemy aircraft.

Confusion and heartbreak haunt the faces of everyone. What stands out is how much furniture people are carrying. They've learnt: if your home isn't bombed or burned, it will be looted or destroyed. Carrying as much as you can has become a survival tactic. Even solar panels are essential, people take them wherever they go. These panels provide power to charge lights and phones. They've become a source of income too: after over eight months of electricity blackouts, people are offering charging services for a fee.

A bicycle passes in front of me, peddled by a thin man in his twenties with pale, tired features. His wife is balanced on the handlebars. Their two sleepy children, cheeks flushed by sunburn, sit on the rack at the back. A small bundle of belongings hangs from the bike frame, swaying as the family heads northward.

I stand frozen for a while, watching as the road swallows the fluttering black of the mother's cloak. That image could win international awards, if only a skilled photographer could capture it: the whole story of our displacement, told in one picture.

I smile bitterly, thinking how a single photo turned the whole world against the Vietnam War. Our tragedies, too, have filled the world's newspapers, websites and social media platforms. But our slaughter hasn't stopped. It's as if the world's eyes have grown used to our suffering. And if our suffering no longer shocks anyone, what's the point of sharing it? What's the point of photos and facts if they don't change our reality?

I keep walking, trying to forget this picture of our misery, and begin to hum the song 'Leftist Love' by Ziad Rahbani:[5]

With nothing at all, I love you
There's no money in this love
No coins, no land, no jewelry
With nothing at all, I love you

May 12, 2024

Today, my father is lamenting the cost of a gas cylinder: 1,200 shekels. And that's *if* you can find one. This isn't the first time gas has run out. It's an ongoing crisis: sometimes easing, sometimes worsening. Most people now cook over wood fires, the price of which has also rocketed. My mother suggests buying ready-made falafel discs. Breakfasting on store-bought falafel saves gas, so it's a good option.

The falafel vendor on our street is one of our displaced relatives. Back in Gaza City, he upholstered furniture in Sheikh Radwan market. But after his displacement, he started selling falafel in the South. His wood-baked and quickly-fried falafel have become popular. People form long queues to buy from his stall. He even has a theme tune, chanted by the children:

Abu Awni
Oh brave one
Prince of falafel

Gas, bread, fresh water and salty water are the necessities we strive to secure during this, our *eighth* displacement.

We've rented an apartment in al-Mawasi, in the West of Rafah, from a simple farmer named Abu Ibrahim Zorab. The farmer is a man in his forties, a father of three girls and four boys. His quiet, rural lifestyle impresses me: feeding his family from his land's produce, unconcerned by the lack of nearby services. Now, this bucolic setting shelters hundreds of thousands of displaced people.

My mother has made a friend: Umm Muhammad, a lively woman with a lovely voice and a charming accent. She bakes bread for the camp's women on a mud oven which her two young sons have built for her. Lately, we've been sending her our flour, yeast and salt, which she returns as baked bread. Our whole family agrees that hers is the tastiest bread we'd ever eaten.

Each day, from the window, I vigilantly await the arrival of the water lorry. Usually, the noise of the crowd lets me know it's coming before I see it.

When the lorry arrives, I call out to my siblings, and they run with empty barrels in their arms to one of the five hoses dangling from the lorry's back and sides. Dozens of people gather — children, women, men — all with their own containers, eager to secure enough drinking water to last until the next visit.

The lorry only comes once a day, and its supply doesn't meet everyone's needs. One time, the lorry was late. People waited, barrels in hand, aimless and worried.

Finally, the lorry appeared, emerging like a sunrise or a bride at a wedding. Cheering, whistling and chanting filled the camp as children clung to the sides of the lorry. How quickly people's expressions changed.

I laughed and cried at the same time: grateful for the water, but saddened to realise how much our lives had changed, how we'd started to celebrate the barest of essentials.

January 1, 2025

Today is my daughter Rusal's sixth birthday. Rusal: my sweet, delicate child, growing up amid the harshness of war.

I've come to accept that my children bear no blame for the world they were born into. I've promised myself that, no matter what, I will bring them moments of happiness.

After visiting a friend to offer condolences for her husband's passing, I hurry to prepare a birthday cake for Rusal. But as I gather the ingredients, I realise I have no eggs.

I don't hesitate. I go out, searching the market, stopping at every vendor, asking: 'Do you have an egg? I only need one.'

The answers are the same:

'They're out of stock.'

'They're too expensive.'

'We don't sell them any more.'

I visit dozens of vendors, refusing to give up. Rusal can't be disappointed on her birthday.

As the sun sets and exhaustion sets in, an elderly vendor sees the fatigue on my face. He approaches me, and asks why I'm so desperately searching for an egg.

'It's my little girl's birthday,' I tell him. 'I just want to bake her a cake.'

He smiles. 'You're determined to celebrate, even in the midst of war? That is beautiful.'

He slips into his small tent, and returns with a single egg.

'This is the last one I have,' he says, handing it to me. 'Happy birthday to your daughter.'

Tears well in my eyes. I thank him with all my heart, and hurry home as darkness settles on the city.

My mother has been anxiously awaiting my return. The moment she sees me, she scolds: 'Where were you? You were gone so long, and it's already dark!'

I hold up the egg, and she understands.

We get to work, rushing to prepare the cake. We know it needs a few more eggs, but we make do, using vinegar as a substitute.

When the cake is finally ready, our small family gathers in our tiny, asbestos-walled room. We huddle around and sing

'Happy Birthday'. There are no candles to blow out, but candles don't matter. What matters is that we're together.

Without hesitation, Rusal says, 'I wish for the war to end. I wish we could see Baba again.'

Her joyful eyes melt away all my exhaustion, all my sorrow. No matter how cruel the war, our love will always give us something worth holding onto.

NOTES

1. Israeli forces bombed al-Ahli Baptist Hospital in Gaza City on October 17, 2023, killing hundreds of displaced people who had been using the hospital for shelter.

2. Hiba Abu Nada: Poet and novelist. Her poem 'Not Just Passing', was published posthumously in *Arablit Quarterly*, translated by Huda Fakhreddine. It contains the lines: 'O little light in me, don't die / even if all the galaxies of the world / close in.'

3. PUBG: A frenetic multiplayer videogame, in which players compete to be the last person alive in a warzone.

4. As reported by Sky News, Benny Gantz, a member of Israel's War Cabinet, told a conference of Jewish American leaders on February 18, 2024, that Israeli forces were preparing to invade the southern Gazan city of Rafah by the end of Ramadan that year (April 9 onwards). At the time, Rafah had become a refuge for over a million Palestinians (more than four times the city's pre-genocide population), including many of those forcibly displaced from their homes in the North. On March 9, then-President Joe Biden told MSNBC that an invasion of Rafah would constitute a 'red line', for his country's support for Israel, adding '[we] cannot have 30,000 more Palestinians dead'. Eight weeks later, the Israeli invasion of Rafah began.

5. Ziad Rahbani: Lebenese songwriter and playwright, known for his communist politics.

EDITORS' NOTE

IT WAS OUR HOPE, in editing this collection, that a lasting cease-fire would mark a natural endpoint to the diaries of Batool, Sondos, Nahil and Ala'a. The actions of Israel have proved otherwise.

On May 4, 2025, six weeks after unilaterally breaking the ceasefire and 63 days after blocking all food and humanitarian aid from entering the Strip, Israel's Security Cabinet unanimously approved plans for a new ground invasion of Gaza, codenamed Operation Gideon's Chariot, which commenced on May 19.

Many of the hopes expressed in the diary entries for early 2025 have been extinguished or deferred. The triumphant return of displaced people to the North (so celebrated by Sondos and Nahil) has been reversed by new evacuation orders. The 400 aid distribution sites of the UN-led aid distribution network, which helped distribute food and resources through much of the genocide, have been replaced by just four Israeli- and US-run sites under the banner of the 'Gaza Humanitarian Foundation'—sites described by the UN as 'a deliberate attempt to weaponise aid' and by Israeli soldiers as 'killing fields' (*Haaretz*) in which orders are regularly given to open fire on unarmed civilians, killing at least 549 Palestinians and injuring over 4,000 in the first month of the GHF's operation alone (Al Jazeera), including over 2,000 children (Save The Children).

On June 25, five days before this book went to print, the United Nations Office for the Coordination of Humanitarian

Affairs (OCHA) reported that 82.6% of the Gaza Strip was under Israeli control, either through displacement orders or as part of Israeli-militarised zones.

Just today, an Israeli attack on the seaside Al-Baqa Cafeteria in northern Gaza City — a hub for journalists and a refuge for many displaced people — killed 33 Palestinians, including the photojournalist Ismail Abu Hatab and the artist Amina 'Frans' al-Salmi, and wounded the reporter Bayan Abu Sultan (Al Jazeera). Since the start of the genocide, Israeli forces have killed over 227 journalists, according to the Office of the UN High Commissioner for Human Rights (OHCHR); they have assassinated writers and artists, including Refaat Alareer and Hiba Abu Nada, and completly destroyed universities and arts centres, including the Islamic University of Gaza and the Rashad Shawa Cultural Centre.

This clear pattern of targeted assaults on journalists, artists and academics has been simultaneously denied by the Israeli military and — as evidenced on occasions including the assassinations of the journalists Ismail al-Ghoul and Rami al-Rifi — openly admitted and bragged about on the IDF's official twitter account.

Batool, Sondos, Nahil and Ala'a remain in Gaza, safe at the time of printing.

They continue to write.

June 30, 2025

TIMELINE OF EVENTS

This is a non-exhaustive list of events referred to in the diaries. It is not a complete history of the Israeli genocide in Gaza.

1947–1949
The Nakba
A series of massacres committed by Zionist militias, leading to the displacement of 750,000 Palestinians, the ethnic cleansing and destruction of over 500 villages, the murder of 15,000 Palestinians and the Israeli occupation of almost all Palestinian land (with the exception of Gaza, the West Bank and East Jerusalem).

2007
Following the election of Hamas in 2006, the Israeli occupation tightened its blockade of the Gaza Strip, imposing restrictions on trade, free movement and access to the Mediterranean Sea.

2023
October
7th: Hamas's al-Qassam Brigades launch a surprise attack on Israeli military bases and settlements in the territory around the northeast border, as widely discussed elsewhere.

9th: Israeli airstrikes destroy the Islamic University in Gaza City.

13th: Israeli forces issue displacement orders to 1.1 million Gazans living in the north of the Strip, including the entirety of Gaza City. These orders give Palestinians only 24 hours to evacuate south of Wadi Gaza.

19th: An Israeli airstrike targets the Church of Saint Porphyrius, which is sheltering both Christian and Muslim families, killing eighteen people, including a three-month-old baby.

20th: An Israeli airstrike kills the poet and novelist Hiba Abu Nada, author of *Oxygen Is Not For The Dead*.

23rd: Israeli forces shell al-Ahli Baptist Hospital, murdering hundreds of displaced people who had been using the hospital for shelter. The bombing is the first major attack on a hospital during the genocide.

25th: The family of the prominent Al Jazeera journalist Wael al-Dahdouh are assassinated in Nuseirat refugee camp alongside 21 other Palestinians. Among the dead are al-Dahdouh's wife, Amna; his children Mahmoud (fifteen) and Sham (seven); and his grandson Adam (eighteen months). Al-Dahdouh's family had complied with Israel's forced displacement orders on October 13 and evacuated south of Wadi Gaza, they were nonetheless targeted.

November
18th–22nd: Israeli forces besiege al-Shifa Hospital, destroying a cardiac ward.

23rd–30th: A temporary truce sees the release of both Palestinian and Israeli captives. Within hours of the truce starting, Israeli forces attack and kill Palestinians returning to their homes in the North.

December
6th: An Israeli airstrike kills the poet and educator Dr Refaat Alareer.
17th: Israeli forces bomb the YMCA in Gaza City.

2024

March

6th: Satellite imagery reveals the formal construction of the Netzarim Corridor: a two-mile-wide Israeli-controlled separation of the north and south of the Strip.

18th: Israeli forces besiege al-Shifa Hospital for the second time.

April

1st: Israeli forces leave al-Shifa Hospital, having killed, injured or detained 1500 Palestinians including medical staff and critically ill patients.

May

6th: Israeli forces begin a ground offensive in the southern city of Rafah, seizing and closing the Rafah Crossing.

11th: Israeli forces besiege Jabalia Refugee Camp.

July

31st: Israeli forces assassinate Ismail Haniyeh, the political leader of Hamas, in the Iranian capital Tehran.

October

6th: Israeli forces besiege Jabalia Refugee Camp for the second time.

16th: Hamas leader Yahya Sinwar is killed in a battle with Israeli forces.

December

27th: Israeli forces raid Kamal Adwan Hospital and kidnap its director, Dr Hussam Abu Safiya.

2025

January

19th: A ceasefire comes into effect between Hamas and Israel.

27th: Israel withdraws from the Netzarim Corridor, allowing displaced Gazans to return to the North in large numbers, many finding their homes in ruin.

March
18th: Israel unilaterally breaks off the ceasefire with a series of simultaneous airstrikes, killing 400 Palestinians in a single night.

GAZA STRIP

Jabalia Camp

JABALIA

BEIT HANOUN

Al Shati Camp

GAZA
CITY

BEIT LAHIA

WADI GAZA

Nuseirat Camp

ZAWAYDA

NETZARIM
CORRIDOR

DEIR AL-BALAH

Deir al Balah Camp

Bureij Camp

HAMAD CITY

Maghazi Camp

Al-Rasheed Road

Salah al-Din Road

KHAN
YOUNIS

AL MAWASI

Khan
Younis
Camp

AL QARARA

KHUZA'A

Rafah Camp

RAFAH

RAFAH
CROSSING

KAREM SHALOM
CROSSING

GAZA CITY

Sobhet Khair
Displacement Camp
Al-Karamah
Towers
Al-Shati
Camp
Al-Nasr
Jabalia
Camp
Sheikh
Radwan
Jabalia
North
Rimal
South
Rimal
Al-Daraj
Toufah
Al-Sabra
Sheikh
Ejleen
Tel
al-Hawa
Old
City
Shuja'iyya
Al-Zaytoun

North Rimal
Al-Nasr Street
Al-Shifa
Medical
Compound
Al-Nasr
Omar Muktar
Street
Al-Wadha
Street
Al-Rasheed
Street
South Rimal
Al-Jala'a
Street
Shawa & Hosari Tower
Al-Wafa
Displacement
Camp
Islamic
University

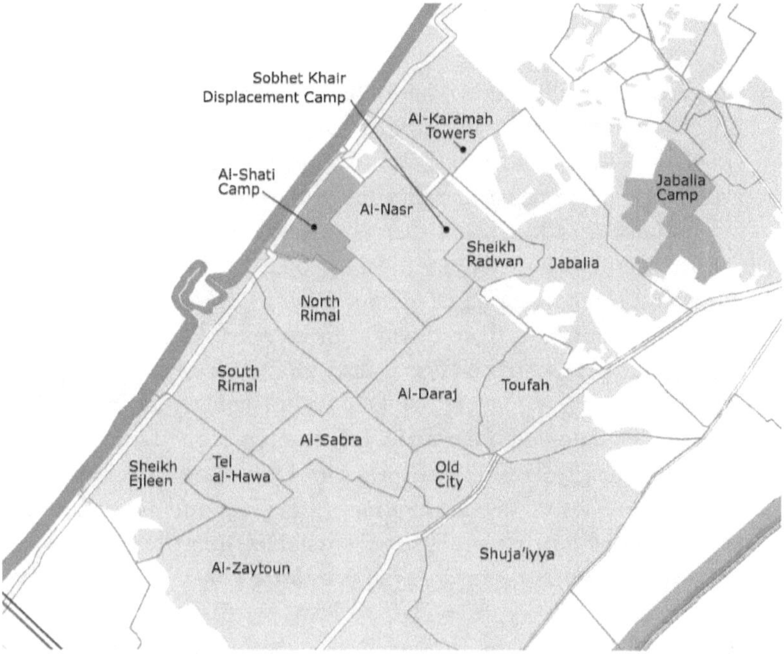

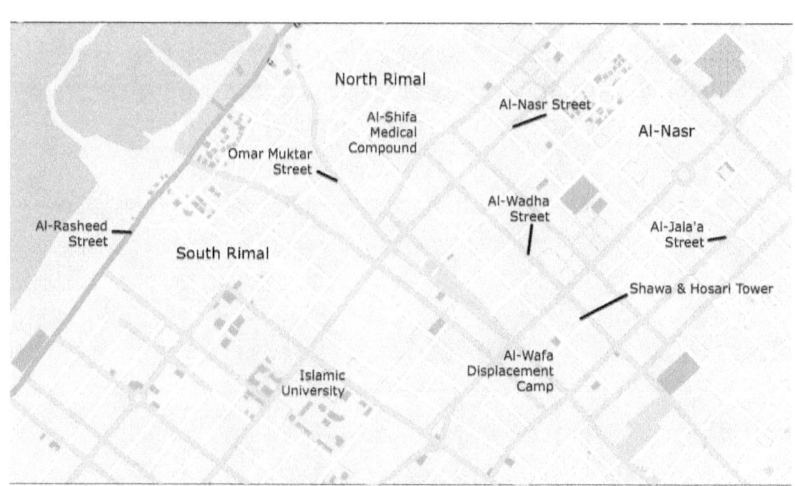

ACKNOWLEDGEMENTS

Edited extracts from these diaries have previously been published in the following places. Sondos Sabra: 7 Oct 23, 16 Jan 24, 12 May 24 & 1 Oct 24 in 'Letter from Gaza: A Year of Devastation', *The New Statesman*, 7 Oct 24; 7 Oct 23, 13 Oct 23, 14 Nov 23, 16 Jan 24, 12 May 24, 1 Oct 24 & 31 Oct 24 in 'Diaries from North Gaza: One Woman's Story of Survival', *Mondoweiss*, 29 Nov 24; 6 January 24 in *Writing Behind the Lines: Diaries from the War on Gaza* (Palestinian Ministry of Culture). Nahil Mohana: 7-29 Oct 23 in 'War Diary', *AGNI*, 31 May 24; 17 Nov 23, 20 Nov 23, 5 Dec 23, 31 Dec 23, 14 Jan 24, 23 Jan 24 in 'Escaping Genocide: Diary of a Life in Gaza', *The Literary Hub*, 27 Aug, 2024; 30 Jan 24-15 Apr 24 in 'Don't Look Back: Diary of a Life in Gaza', *The Literary Hub*, 4 Sep 24; and 15-16 Jan 24 in 'I Live in Gaza. This is What We will Do After the Ceasefire', *The Washington Post*, 21 Jan 25; 6-20 Nov 24, 1-5 Jan 25, 26 Jan 25, 28 Jan-2 Feb 25 in *AGNI*, 19 May 25. Ala'a Obaid: 13-19 Oct 23 (in Arabic) in *Writing Behind the Lines*; 23 Feb 24 (in Arabic) in *Disturbing Flashbacks* (Palestinian Ministry of Culture). Extracts from Sondos, Nahil and Ala'a's diaries were performed at the Barbican, London, 14 September 24. Extracts from Batool, Sondos, Nahil and Ala'a's diaries were performed at the Belgrade Theatre, Coventry, 14 June 2025.

SPECIAL THANKS

The publishers would like to thank: Nuradin Abdi, Ahmed Adnan, Ashjan Ajour, Leila Ashraf-Carr, Grant Archer, Julie-Yara Atz, Divya Avula, Mollie Balshaw, Isabella Barber, Rebekah Beasley, Nasima Begum, Kingsley Ben-Adir, Christian Berger, Willie Black, Kat Boon, Nafeesah Butt, Jeremy Corbyn, Marwan Darweish, Nabil Elouahabi, Dr Mona El-Farra, Musheir El-Farra, Qasem El-Farra, Jude FireSong, George Forster, Sophia Gardiner, Baha Ghalayini, Sondos Ghalayini, Mohammed Ghalayini, Matt Greaves, Noor Hadid, Rania Abu Hamida, Omar Robert Hamilton, Chris Harker, Vibeke Harper, Iyad Hayatleh, Abbey Heffer, Noor Hemani, Leila Herandi, Firas Ibrahim, Mella Ioana, Rebeca González Izquierdo, Maria Jackson, Ramsey Janini, Adele Jordan, Salma Khadid, Nardine Khalil, Kiays Khalil, Shamshad Khan, Niloo-Far Khan, Masa Khawaja, Loukia Koumi, Ciara Leeming, Robert Lizar, Nikki Mailer, Haru Marui, Danielle McIlven, Adie Mormech, Linda Nagy, Dalloul Al Neder, Rania Al Neder, Ahmed Nehad, Chris Neophytou, John Nicholson, Nora Parr, Maxine Peake, Nirmal Puwar, Sama Rantisi, David Renton, Atef Abu Saif, Zaki El-Salahi, Davina Shah, Hossam Abu Shammallah, Kamila Shamsie, Nada Shawa, Talal Abu Shawish, Meg Shear, Hind Shoufani, Ryann Sowden, Zarah Sultana, Norma Turner, Ricardo Vilela, Bea Vilela, Cristina Viti, Yusra Warsama, Naomi Wimborne-Idrissi, Freya Wysocki, everyone at Respond Crisis Translation, Modern Poetry in Translation, Tenement Press and all the artists who withdrew their work from HOME's Open exhibition in April 2024. Special thanks to Dani Abulhawa, Marcia Lynx, Ayah Najadat, Ninutsa Nadirashvili, Nuala Shaar, Trudi Shaw, David Sue and, of course, Batool Abu Akleen, Sondos Sabra, Nahil Mohana and Ala'a Obaid: this book wouldn't exist without you.

BASMA GHALAYINI was born in Khan Younis and raised in Gaza City, Her previous translations have been published by Commonwealth Writers, Deep Vellum Press and Comma Press (*Banthology*, *The Book of Cairo*, *The Book of Ramallah* and others). She is the editor of *Palestine + 100: Stories from a Century After the Nakba* (Comma, 2019). She currently lives in Manchester.

RESPOND CRISIS TRANSLATION is an abolitionist language justice organisation providing emergency translation services and correcting harmful mistranslations in media reports. Respond's work on *Voices of Resistance* was led by Ayah Najadat.